Take Your Performance Up-A-Notch

Mastering the Six Hats of the Continuously Improving Salesperson

Dave Kahle
The DaCo Corporation
Grand Rapids, MI

This publication is designed to provide accurate and authoritative information in regard to the subject matter covered. It is sold with the understanding that the publisher is not engaged in rendering legal, accounting or other professional service. If legal advice or other expert assistance is required, the services of a competent professional person should be sought.

ISBN: 0-9647042-1-8
Copyright 2002, Dave Kahle
All rights reserved.
Printed in the United States of America.

This publication may not be reproduced, stored in a retrieval system, or transmitted in whole or in part, in any form or by any means, electronic, mechanical, photocopying, recording, or otherwise, without the prior written permission of the author.

Take Your Performance Up-A-Notch
Table of Contents

Introduction.. v

Chapter One: Selling in the Information Age...................... 1
Presents a sobering look at some of the trends that define the Information Age and their impact on salespeople and their customers.

Chapter Two: Introduction to the Six Hats........................19
Describes the rationale for the Six Hats, and the concept of principles, processes and tools as the components of a competency.

Chapter Three: The First Hat – Astute Planner...................31
Describes the power of collecting useful information, and shows you how to collect useful information about your customers and your competitors.

Chapter Four: Astute Planner – Part II............................47
Presents the principles and processes for creating powerful territory, account and sales plans.

Chapter Five: Using the Six Hats to Take Your Performance Up-A-Notch 67
This mini-chapter addresses the common problem of "My customers don't have much time for me," with solutions based on the Six Hats.

Chapter Six: The Second Hat – Trusted Friend 71
Describes the power of positive relationships to provide a salesperson with a competitive advantage, and presents principles and processes for causing your customers to become comfortable with you.

Chapter Seven: Trusted Friend – Part II: Gaining Your Customer's Trust and Respect 93
Presents principles and processes for developing these aspects of a relationship. Includes the "Nine commandments for ethical salespeople."

Chapter Eight: Using the Six Hats to Take Your Performance Up-A-Notch 109
"Voice mail is driving me crazy!" This mini-chapter shows how to use the Six Hats to deal with this vexing problem.

Chapter Nine: The Third Hat – Effective Consultant 113
Presents the concept of becoming a consultant to your customers by knowing them better than anyone else, and then provides principles and processes for doing so.

Chapter Ten: Effective Consultant – Part II: Using Questions Effectively 137
Shows you how to use questions to understand your customers at deeper levels and provides "Seven rules for constructive listening."

Chapter Eleven: Using the Six Hats to Take Your Performance Up-a-Notch 155
This mini-chapter shows you how to use the Six Hats to deal with a high-potential account in which a competitor is firmly entrenched.

Chapter Twelve: The Fourth Hat – Skillful Influencer 161
Describes the concept of sales as a set of step-by-step processes, and focuses on the principles and processes to make a powerful sales presentation.

Chapter Thirteen: Skillful Influencer – Part II: Closing the Sale 185
Presents principles and processes for mastering this most crucial aspect of selling.

Chapter Fourteen: Using the Six Hats to Take Your Performance Up-A-Notch 203
Your customers are confused because they have more choices than ever before. It's difficult to get them to make decisions. This mini-chapter shows you how to use the Six Hats to succeed in this situation.

Chapter Fifteen: The Fifth Hat – Adept Human Resource Manager 209
The resource you mange is you! This chapter presents powerful principles and processes for proactively moving in positive directions: goal-setting, focusing on your strengths, and "Ten Commandments for Good Sales Time Management."

Chapter Sixteen: Adept Human Resource Manager – Part II 235
To be effective in the high stress Information Age, you need to know how to handle the negative forces pressing on you. The chapter presents principles and processes for handling failure, adversity, information overload, and negative thinking.

Chapter Seventeen: Using the Six Hats to Take Your Performance Up-A-Notch 261
This mini-chapter shows you how to use the Six Hats to deal with the expansion of paperwork, details and "other stuff" that threatens to squeeze out your selling time.

Chapter Eighteen: The Sixth Hat – Master Learner 265
Becoming good at continuously growing, developing, and changing yourself is the ultimate success competency for the Information Age. This chapter presents principles and tools to achieve mastery of that competency.

Chapter Nineteen: Master Learner – Part II 281
Describes our trademark Menta-Morphosis™ process for continuous personal growth.

Chapter Twenty: Using the Six Hat to Take Your Performance Up-A-Notch 313
How to use the Six Hats to deal with constant changes within your organization.

Introduction

I love sales. No, I'm not crazy, I'm blessed. The world of sales has provided me a career with a lifetime of challenge, unlimited opportunity to express my individuality, to make a good living, to grow as a human being, to create relationships and friendships, and to exercise all of my gifts and talents. Very few people are blessed with all of that.

I suppose it was my father who planted the seed of interest in me. He was a salesperson for a number of years, and then later became a branch manager. So, when I was a teenager and was offered a job in retail sales, it was easy for me to say yes. Sales ran in the family.

That experience of selling men's clothing in an expensive retail store was my initiation into sales. There I learned I had a knack for sales. I became the leading salesperson in my store. Later, I took another baby step forward when, during the summers in my college days, I went to work at a company that sold housewares and groceries to housewives on a route. That put me in an environment where I was outside seeing people, not just waiting for them to come into the store. Again, I met with some success, and won a scholarship as the outstanding summer employee in a three-district area.

With that success under my belt, and after a few years as a teacher, I was ready for my first full time sales position, selling capital equipment to school systems. Eighteen months later I was the number one salesperson in the country and ready for a new challenge. Off to selling surgical staplers to doctors in the operating room. After a dismal start, I made more money than I thought possible, and eventually left to go into business for myself, selling motivational and training products. Two years later, I sold that company, and went to work for a sales recruiter, "selling people" to sales managers. That led me to my final full time sales position, selling hospital supplies, where I again became the number one salesperson in the country.

In 1988, I began my current career as a professional speaker, sales trainer and sales consultant. Since then, through my seminars and consulting projects, I've interacted with literally thousands of salespeople and their managers.

In this checkered variety of sales experiences, I have learned some of the wisdom that I hope to pass on to you in this book. My focus is on helping establish salespeople take their performance up a notch. I've learned that the difference between a great salesperson and a mediocre one is often just a little bit of difference applied in some very specific places. I'd like to show you where those differences are, and how to apply a little bit of effort to make a huge difference.

And I'd like to go one step further. My intention is to make it easy for you to understand and implement that wisdom. As a sales trainer, I know that the biggest obstacle to sales performance is not knowing what to do, it's doing it! So, from the very beginning, this book was designed to provide a system that would be doable. Everything, from the title at the beginning to the summary at the end, has been designed to make it easy for you to implement.

You'll find four major components in this book which all support the objective of providing you an easy-to-implement system. First, you'll see "principles." Principles are bedrock, fundamental observations of deep truths. They express ageless truths about human beings. Regardless of the ebb and flow at the surface of your life, principles remain unchanged. You can count on them to be true. So if you can uncover the key truths, or the principles that relate to selling, you'll have a foundation on which you can build for the rest of your sales career, continuously moving your performance up one more notch.

That the understanding of key principles is an important step toward success and maturity can be substantiated by a wide variety of sources. Look at Steven Covey's great concept of "principle-centered leadership." Or review the work of an even more widely read author. Peruse the Bible, and you'll discover the unveiling of principle after principle concerning human life.

While understanding principles is an important step, it's almost as important that you are building on the *right* principles. For example, you may argue for the existence of a sales principle that states, "People are easily duped." While that principle may be true, it is *not* one on which you want to build a sales career. In this book, I've attempted to share my observation of the most important principles that effect sales success. Learn them, and you'll be equipped with a wisdom that will serve you well the rest of your life.

Next, you'll notice "processes." Processes are the links that connect your understanding of principles to your behavior. Processes unleash the power of your potential by providing the how-to steps that help you actually implement the principles. They are often lacking in many books, seminars and training programs. Early in my career as a sales trainer and speaker, I had one of my seminar participants tell me "We've heard other people, and they all have good things to say, but they never teach the how to of implementing them. It's always, 'you should do this or you should do that' but never how to. That's what I like about your program. You show us how to."

That emphasis on "how-to" has been a hallmark of my work. I don't consider myself a motivational speaker, but I believe that my presentations are very motivational. That's because I don't focus on emotional issues like many motivational speakers. Rather I show people how to do something. And my experience has taught me that knowing not just what to do, but how to do it is tremendously motivating. So, the major thrust of this book is the "how-to's" -- the processes.

The third component designed to make this material easily doable is the use of simple graphic images. Our minds think in images. I learned a long time ago that if I could connect a concept to a simple graphic image, then my seminar participants would remember it for years, and find it easier to implement. So, you'll find graphic images spread throughout the book, beginning with the title, and moving on to almost every key concept.

Finally, the last component you'll find liberally sprinkled throughout the book is the use of illustrations from my sales experience. People relate to stories, and in my 30 years of selling, I've accumulated a number of them.

So, this combination of principles, processes, graphic images and personal examples are all combined into a system designed to help you make significant, powerful changes in your sales career.

I'm assuming, since you're reading it, that you're either a salesperson or sales manager. This book is for you.

If you're currently a professional salesperson, this book is designed to help you deal with the biggest broad-stroke issue of your career - responding effectively to the changes that are being driven by our culture's transformation to the Information Age. I'm thoroughly convinced that the skills and tactics that may have served you well in the past are being rendered obsolete. I can't number the countless salespeople with whom I have spoken in hundreds of sales training sessions who express pain and confusion over the changes that they are being asked to make.

This book is for you – to help you make the changes you need to make to become successful, ever growing individuals in our new economy.

Or, you may be a new salesperson, looking for shortcuts to success – ways to shorten the inevitable trial and error learning curve.

This book is for you -- to help you grasp the wisdom necessary to become ever more successful so that you might be as privileged as I have been – with a lifetime of challenge and opportunity.

Finally, you may be someone who manages salespeople, looking for insights into the skills and processes to instill in your sales force.

This book is for you, to provide you a simple and powerful system to inculcate into your sales force to help them reach your goals for them.

Regardless of your position, it's my hope that your life will be just a bit richer and fuller as a result of the changes this book prompts you to make. This book is for you.

Chapter One:
Selling in the Information Age

What in the world is going on?

The Information Age is here. And it has brought with it transformational changes in the way that successful salespeople must go about their jobs.

If you're an experienced salesperson, you're going to need to make some significant changes in the way that you do your job. If you're just beginning your sales career, you need to understand what it's going to take to be successful. If you're a sales manager, you need to know what behaviors to encourage in your team. Regardless of where you're currently at, this book will open the door to success in the Information Age for you. The Six Hats of the continuously improving salesperson hold the answers for each of you.

From my vantage point as a consultant and trainer to a wide variety of industries around the world, I see certain trends moving through our world-wide economy that are causing havoc among businesspeople in general, and salespeople in particular.

The changes coursing through economies around the world are revolutionary, like nothing mankind has seen ever before. And you, the professional salesperson, are caught in the middle of it. The strategies, skills, and concepts that used to work for you are no longer sufficient to assure your success. They may be necessary, but they're not sufficient. The world is just too different.

The new realities of the Information Age require a new paradigm for sales success — as well as a new set of principles, processes, and tools. And that is what the Six Hat Salesperson is all about.

Let's look at some of these characteristics of the Information Age.

Characteristics of the Information Age

Before we can discuss the pressures on salespeople, we need to examine the forces that characterize the Information Age and affect business people around the world.

Imagine each of these forces to be like an ocean current. An ocean current is an incredibly powerful, unseen force - maybe the most powerful force on the planet. Yet, ocean currents are hard to see. We know where they are by observing the effect they have on things around them. We can see the flotsam and jetsam swept along in their path.

So it is with the trends and pressures on salespeople in the Information Age. They are like ocean currents -- powerful, unseen forces coursing through economies and societies around the world, sweeping along everyone in their path: Our customers, our competitors, our companies, even our families.

When two or more ocean currents slam together, they create a treacherous, turbulent stretch of whitewater. So, too, for the trends moving through our economies. Like ocean currents, these trends merge and converge to form a whirlpool of turbulence.

Turbulence may be the most accurate adjective for our world -- the defining characteristic of the Information Age. As professional salespeople, you may sometimes feel like you're hanging on to a piece of driftwood in the middle of permanent whitewater.

Examining each of these currents will help you gain perspective.

The First Current: Rapid, Discontinuous Change

You've probably noticed -- it's an era of warp-speed change. Markets emerge, mature and disappear almost overnight. New competitors appear out of nowhere. Hot new products become obsolete dinosaurs in months. Technologies change in the blink of an eye. Customers change rapidly. Our companies downsize, reengineer and transform. Welcome to the Information Age.

Perhaps "Information Age" is a misnomer. Maybe we should call it the Era of Change. It seems like everywhere we look, the world is changing faster than the images on an MTV music video. Certainly business environments around the world are changing more rapidly than at any time in our history. The problem is that this change is not an event, it's a continuous process. And the pace or rate of that process of change is continuously increasing.

We've always had change. In fact, change may be a definition for life itself. If you're not changing, you're probably dead! I recall, in my days as a field sales rep, being very frustrated with one account. The account had a prime vendor relationship with my arch competitor and, no matter what I did, I couldn't increase my meager business there. I ended up venting my frustrations to my manager who counseled me to "hang in there."

"The only thing you can be sure of," he said, "is that things will change. You need to position yourself to take advantage of those changes when they happen." Events proved him right. My competitor changed salespeople, experienced some service problems, and I had the opening for which I had been waiting.

So, we've always had change. It's the rate of that change that is different now. Things are changing more rapidly than ever before. And the force driving that rate of change is the explosion in the amount of information we're creating. That's why it's called the Information Age. Consider this. In 1900, the total amount of knowledge available to mankind was doubling about every 500 years. Today, it doubles about every two years. That incredibly rapid pace of new knowledge production puts energy into the forces of change at an unprecedented rate.

Some futurists predict that the total amount of information we have today will amount to only less than 5% of that which will be available to us in the year 2010.

It's not knowledge itself that causes change, it's the application of knowledge. We see the application of knowledge in new products, new technologies, new customers, new needs -- all coming at an increasingly rapid rate.

Like it or not, the conclusions, paradigms and core beliefs upon which we based our decisions two years ago are likely to be obsolete today.

Chuck's story is a good example.

Not long ago, Chuck, one of my friends, shocked me by announcing that he had to get out of the business he owned and find another one.

I was stunned. My first thought was, "Why on earth would he need to find a different business?" Chuck was living the American dream. Ten years ago he was a computer repairman who risked everything by leaving his job to develop his own computer repair business. Over the past few years, Chuck had built an efficient, productive business employing 15 people in two locations.

His business had become stable and profitable, he was well regarded by his clients, he had a good, loyal group of employees, and he was enjoying an income probably greater than he ever imagined.

He was relishing the kind of situation about which most people only dream. So why did he need to find a new business?

Here's what he told me. "In five years, I'll be out of business. Manufacturers are continually building computers that are smaller, cheaper and more reliable. It won't be long before you won't repair them -- you'll throw them away like you do a toaster. There won't be a need for the service my business provides."

Chuck's business was a winner in an industry -- micro computer repair -- that will have come and gone in a period of about fifteen years. No matter how effective and productive Chuck was as a businessman, the rapid changes in our economy meant that the long-term prospect for his business was dim. And Chuck was astute enough to recognize that before it was too late.

Two years ago the future looked great for his business. Today, it looks dim. Things have changed. And these changes came about as a result of increased knowledge on the part of the computer manufacturers. Think about it. An IBM PC was a revolutionary product and sold for about $4,500 when it was introduced a few years ago. Today, it probably doesn't even have scrap value.

Things changed. The application of increased knowledge resulted in new products which made that product obsolete. If that was true for the IBM PC and the host of products and variations which followed, think about what may happen to today's hot product. Regardless of how well researched, engineered and manufactured it may be, it could become obsolete and worthless in two years!

One futurist has predicted that, by the year 2020, knowledge will increase at an astounding rate -- doubling every 35 days! What that means for salespeople is that the rapid change affecting almost every aspect of your business -- products, markets, customers, etc. -- will only continue to increase in speed. We are living in a world that is changing more rapidly than anything mankind has experienced ever before. This rapid change, fueled by increasing amounts of information, is, and will continue to be, the primary tenant of the Information Age.

But there's another element to this current of rapid change. Not only is change rapid, but it's unlike anything we've seen before.

Charles Handy, in his book, *The Age of Unreason*, makes a convincing argument that change today is "discontinuous." In other words, it doesn't necessarily evolve out of patterns or trends that we can predict. For example, the three television networks co-existed quite comfortably for years. They competed with one another and gradually changed as the technology and tastes of their audience evolved.

But then, in a matter of a year or two, cable television burst onto the field, and the networks suddenly had hundreds of small stations and networks with which to battle. Their world was turned upside down by a technological development which changed things in a "discontinuous" fashion.

Rapid, discontinuous change. It's the first current surging through our Information Age world.

The Second Current: Relentlessly Growing Complexity

Everywhere we look – every aspect of our business lives – is becoming more and more complex.

The explosion in knowledge means that the products we buy and sell are becoming increasingly complex. Automobiles are a good example. Last spring one of our family cars stopped running. It didn't gradually slow down or signal it's impending demise by running roughly -- it just stopped. Suddenly and without advance warning. It was as if it just announced one day, "I will run no more," and then shut itself down.

No matter what I did, I couldn't get it to start. A look under the hood revealed a complex array of wires and tiny black boxes that were totally new to me. Automobiles had become so complex that I had no idea what those little electronic boxes did. Nor how to fix them.

Just a few years ago that maze of wires and electronics would not have been there, and the car wouldn't have been nearly so intimidating. I could have wiggled a wire, adjusted a carburetor, or done something to revive it.

But the explosion of knowledge and the resulting complexity in my car left me intimidated and totally confused by what I saw under the hood. So, in frustration, I gave up and had the car towed to the dealer. And what did the dealer do to it? The mechanic hooked it up to a computer to tell him what was wrong. The car had become so complex that even the mechanic couldn't diagnose the problem without the assistance of a computer. A victim of rapid change and growing complexity.

This complexity seeps into every area of business, making it more sophisticated and intricate than a few years ago, and assuring that it will be even more so a few years from now.

If you work for a manufacturer, for example, chances are that your product lines are broader and more intricate than a few years ago. Chances are also great that many of those individual products you sell are themselves more sophisticated and complex than a few years ago. If you're with a service company, chances are that the services you sell are more complex and sophisticated than a few years ago. On and on it goes. On the product or service side of your business, it's likely that you are having to deal with considerably more complexity than ever before.

But product complexity is only one part of the relentlessly growing complexity current. Government regulation continues to grow, bringing with it layers of complexity that reach out and effect every area of our business lives.

Think of the great tax reform act of 1990. Or the Americans with Disabilities Act which ushered in an entirely new area of regulation. The number of regulations that business people are expected to follow only continues to grow.

One last source of complexity -- our friends the attorneys. It seems that with every new law school graduate, the chances of getting sued for something increase. And with every lawsuit we read about or hear about, we, of necessity, become more defensive in our practices. Thus the number of "de facto" regulations grows exponentially.

With the US claiming 70 percent of the world's lawyers, the prospect is great for this current to continue to swell.

Look at the tools and processes you use to do your jobs. I'd feel very comfortable in betting that those are far more complex today than they were a few years ago. I suspect that the computers you use, for example, are so complex that you're only using a tiny portion of their potential power. And, before you begin to master them, new updates will keep mastery too far ahead of you to be realistically achievable.

Finally, let's consider the expectations of your customers. I suspect that, in recent years, your customers have come to expect things of you that they didn't even imagine existed a few years ago.

Everywhere you look, every aspect of your job is growing more complex. This relentlessly growing complexity is the second characteristic of our Information Age world.

The Third Current: Constantly Growing Competition/Choices

As a vendor, do you have more competition today than you did three years ago? As a consumer, do you have more choices today than you did a few years ago?

Those two questions represent both sides of another current. As the rate of information expands, we're faced with more and more competition. That competition may or may not be coming from traditional sources, but it certainly is surfacing as growing choices for your customers. This issue of growing competition, or choices, seeps into every area of our life, affecting us in almost everything we do.

Last summer my wife went to Florida for three weeks to help care for her ill father, leaving me home with three of the kids. And that meant grocery shopping. It had been a number of years since I seriously entered the grocery store in search of the family's weekly provisions. I had, of course, run in from time to time to pick up the miscellaneous one or two items that we needed for a special meal or which we had inadvertently run out of in the middle of a recipe. But I hadn't really had the responsibility for purchasing the family's groceries. It had been 15 years since I confronted the grocery store.

Do you realize what has happened in the grocery store in the last 15 years? There, under one roof, is the quintessential example of all the currents we're discussing. If you could have taken a photograph of the grocery store 15 years ago, and compare it to one taken today, you would not recognize the two as being the same facility.

I muddled through the maze of options until I came to the cereal aisle. There, I stopped dead in my tracks! It was a revelation. Literally stacked from the floor to above my head, running the length of the entire row, were hundreds of choices in cereal. I was confused and overwhelmed. I didn't have time to read all the box labels, and every package was designed to pull my attention to it. In frustration, I resorted to... Shredded Wheat!

My very real frustration with all my choices was a simple illustration of the third current surging relentlessly through our society -- constantly growing competition and choices. The overwhelming number of choices that I faced in that grocery aisle wasn't an isolated instance. In almost every area in which we look, under every nook and cranny of our economy, we are faced with an explosion of choices.

It wasn't so long ago that we had a choice of a handful of TV stations, for example. Today we can choose from at least 40. We're currently shopping for a new automobile for my wife. The choices are endless. Do we really need all these brands of cars? I could go on and on with examples, but they are very clearly everywhere you look. Just look at the options on the web – which didn't even exist a couple of years ago. One of my clients remarked to me, and I think he's right, "There's just too much of everything."

There are two sides to this current. On the one hand, it represents increased choices and freedom for consumers. On the other, it brings increased competition for vendors. Cereal and TV stations may be highly visible, and universally recognized, but this trend affects almost every business person.

Competition is increasing for several reasons. There is, first of all, the explosion in alternate sources. For many traditional salespeople, the discount warehouse, mail order cataloger, or telemarketing operations offer new choices to your customers -- other ways to acquire the same products.

The technology revolution means that more and more processes are being "computerized" and the local computer consultant may be offering alternate ways for your customer to handle the same processes.

As countries around the world go through the downsizing trend in response to increased competition, it creates even more competition. Many of the hundreds of thousands of laid-off white collar workers will not find gainful employment in the industry that they left. Their survival strategy will be to start their own businesses.

Here's another source of increasing competition -- overseas competitors. As the world becomes smaller due to improved transportation and communication technology, foreign competitors are entering our markets. I have yet to work with an industry that didn't have a relatively new foreign player involved. And that's true worldwide.

Finally, our rapidly growing knowledge means innovations in technology. And that technology means new choices for consumers, and new sources of competition for vendors.

Ask yourself these simple questions. Do you have more competition today than you had a few years ago? Do you expect to see more competition in the future? This rapidly expanding competition and options is another of the characteristics of our Information Age world.

The Fourth Current: Constraints on Time

A friend called recently with an invitation for us to spend an evening together. As we compared calendars, we discovered that it was three weeks before my wife and I had an evening in which we were both free!

Unfortunately, that was no isolated event. Our lives have become so full, and so scheduled, that we have very little "free time." I believe we're very typical. Franklin Planners, daytimers and electronic calendars have become ubiquitous in business circles -- a symptom of the growing number of commitments we make. When was the last time you made an appointment with someone who didn't have to wade through pages of commitments in an elaborately detailed calendar, or had to consult an electronic version of the same? As we've become more aware of time, and more committed to using it wisely, we also use it more fully, and leisure time is rapidly becoming a shrinking, precious commodity. Unfortunately, work time is increasing at the expense of family and leisure time.

And our guilt is rising in direct proportion -- we're all trying to cram more productivity into the time we have. The extra hours and leisure minutes we used to use to consider some strategy or situation have disappeared. We're in the quick solution, rapid fix mode -- all due to the increasing pressure on our time.

But, regardless of what is happening to other people, the really important question is, "Is this happening to you?"

Ask yourself this question. "Do I have more pressure on my time today than I did a few years ago?" And, if so,

"Do I realistically expect to get more time, or less time, in the near future?"

If your answer to the last question is "less time," then you can personally relate to the current. Constraints on time is the fourth current swirling through the world of the Information Age salesperson.

These four currents are surging through our society creating whirlpools of confusion and uncertainty -- an incredibly turbulent time. Salespeople, like you, are being overwhelmed by these forces.

Implications for Salespeople

Every day, professional salespeople face new challenges and obstacles brought on by the rapid change that characterizes our entry into the Information Age.

The professional salesperson caught in the middle of this turbulence feels like he/she's being spun around in a whirlpool of confusion and uncertainty. The strategies and skills which have served you well in the past are no longer sufficient.

Over the last few years, in almost every sales training series or seminar that I have presented, I've asked the participating salespeople to think about these trends and then to brainstorm what they see as implications of these trends for them. These professional salespeople have routinely identified a consistent set of challenges. Here's the consolidated list:

Time management
Salespeople must become more effective in the use of their time. With the constant pressure on margins brought on by increasing competition, there's less and less room for slop.

Salespeople are going to have to become adept at using their time in the most effective and efficient ways possible.

✡ Productivity

Salespeople must become more productive than ever before. It is not enough just to sell, you must now sell efficiently and effectively. The ubiquitous competition in every industry means that pressures on prices and profits will continue to grow. It is inevitable that companies will strive to find efficiencies that allow them to operate profitably on lower prices. Salespeople will no longer be immune from the search for productivity.

✡ Focus on the customer

As the perceived differences between products melt away in the minds of the customer, it will be more and more important for the salesperson to understand the customer's needs, wants, interests, problems, objectives and motivations. Instead of focusing on the product, successful Information Age salespeople will focus on the customer.

✡ More training and education

Products will come and go, programs will last for awhile and grow obsolete, services will be eclipsed by the evolving needs of the customer. The salesperson equipped with today's knowledge – whether it be products, processes or programs – will find himself equipped to deal with a world that no longer exists. The Information Age salesperson will have to learn and grow constantly, gaining competency with an ever changing set of products, services and programs.

✦ More technologically astute

Clearly technology now provides a means of growing productivity for the outside salesperson. And, like technology in every other field, it will continue to evolve. The salesperson will need to easily absorb the latest and greatest improvements in hardware and software, or risk being eclipsed by the competition.

All these implications reflect pressures on you -- the salesperson -- from the internal sources – your products and your company. There is, though, another set of pressures that have just as sobering implications. These are pressures on your customers.

🌐 Implications Resulting from Pressures on Your Customers

The sobering truth is that your customers live in the same world you do. They labor to stay afloat in the turbulent environment just like you do. Their worlds are more pressured, their time more precious, their lives more complex, their markets more competitive – just like yours.

This truth about your customers – that they live in the same world you live in – brings with it another whole set of implications for the Information Age salesperson. Let's look at each of the four currents from that perspective and consider the indirect implications on professional salespeople.

Rapid, discontinuous change

This means that your customers are quite likely to change some of the salient dynamics of their business. They could drop product lines, open new market segments, restructure, and transform just like your company. Your customers will be a moving target.

You'll have to master good information just to stay current. Not only that, but the individuals on whom you call are liable to transform and migrate faster than ever. The days of calling on the same person for 10 years are rapidly drawing to a close. Information Age salespeople will have to master the skills of building relationships quickly with a wide range of ever-changing individuals.

Relentlessly growing competition/options

That means that your customers probably have more competition in their businesses than ever. And that means that their businesses are more in jeopardy than ever before. You will have to be sensitive to the ebb and flow of their top line.

But they will have more options than ever before also. Which means that you will need to be more sensitive to your customer's preferences and intricacies so that you'll be able to position your product or service favorably in the light of the other ways your customers could satisfy their needs. Instead of focusing on your product or service, you'll have to focus on the customer.

Complexity

Your customers' job is becoming more difficult. They are becoming overwhelmed with all the information they need to make good decisions. If you are going to win a respected place in their choices, you'll need to be a source of good, useful information to help them deal with the growing complexities of their jobs. You'll need to become their Shredded Wheat.

Constraints on time

Constraints on time effect your customers in a number of ways. First, the days of stopping in without an appointment are over. Their days are just too structured and full to allow that. Secondly, your customers will have less time to make decisions about the products and services you sell, so you'll need to be more effective in your selling, compressing the time spent in the sales cycle.

So, we're in the Information Age. To a professional salesperson, that means that pressures of change, complexity, competition, and constraints on time will pressure you directly, as well as indirectly through your customers.

It's a time ripe with intense danger and rich in opportunity. The danger is that these pressures will make your job much more difficult. You may have to radically transform yourself to become effective. The skills necessary to be successful in the turbulent environment of the Information Age are far more sophisticated than those necessary to get by a few years go. If you're an experienced professional salesperson, the danger is that you may not unlearn habits from the past, and then learn the new skills you need.

The opportunity lies in the fact that if you understand and implement an effective set of principles and processes, you'll be far more successful than your bewildered competition. You will be equipped for a lifetime of success in the permanent whitewater of the Information Age.

The difference between the two are the Six Hats of the Information Age salesperson.

Chapter Two:
Introduction to the Six Hats

My first professional sales position began with six weeks of intense sales training. I lived in a hotel in Mill Valley, California, with five other salespeople. We spent eight hours a day presenting a memorized pitch in front of a video camera, and then critiquing one another until we were able to present it perfectly. We learned how to sell that product.

A few years later, in another sales position, I spent another six weeks in training – this time it was the other coast, New York City. The products were different, but the drill was similar -- learn the pitch and memorize the right words for all the anticipated situations. Learn them word for word, and you'll be well on your way to sales success.

That way of training salespeople -- and the approach to selling that it generated -- worked well then, but not any more. There was a time when a professional salesperson could "learn the pitch." There was a formula for selling any product or service. Focus on the product, learn the presentation, apply it consistently, and you could be successful.

The focus was on the product and the presentation. The concept was that our product is so unique, so full of features, that all we have to do is accurately describe them to you, and you'll have to buy! Sales success was a matter of voicing a predetermined set of words for a finite number of situations.

Most sales literature expounded upon the same concept. Learn these 24 special closes, and you'll be successful! Memorize these 15 magic bullets! Use these special words! By far the overwhelming preponderance of what passes as sales training today is merely information about products or services, or pat answers and magic bullets from sales gurus who generalize from their limited experience in their industries.

Those types of approaches to sales worked well when we lived in a slower, less competitive age. You really could identify the two or three most common objections for your product, and memorize the most effective responses. And you'll be in good shape for years. But, as we learned in the last chapter, those days are gone!

The world is changing more rapidly than ever. Today's pitch is obsolete tomorrow, and memorized solutions, like hi-tech products, are obsolete in a matter of a few months. As soon as you master the formula, something changes -- the situation, your customer, the competition, or even your own product or program. Focusing on the product and the presentation leads to frustrating obsolescence. Searching the literature for packaged solutions is a never ending journey through a maze. Expecting any single approach to be applicable to a constantly changing customer base is no longer effective.

Salespeople need a new approach for the Information Age -- an approach to their profession that will allow them to change with the environment. That's what *The Six Hat Salesperson* is all about. Here's the idea. If you rely on memorized pitches, magic "closes," and single approaches, you limit yourself to a finite number of situations. It's more important to master certain principles you can apply to countless numbers of situations, and to master certain processes which you can use to create your own pitches, to identify your own solutions. If you focus on principles and processes which you can use to create your own solutions, you'll be equipped to deal with any situation that comes up, no matter how frequently the dynamics of that situation changes.

You've heard the saying, "Give a man a fish, and you've fed him for a day. Teach him how to fish, and you've fed him for a lifetime."

That's what we're talking about. Memorize the pitch, focus on the product or the presentation, rely on one way of selling, and you may be successful for a moment. Focus on the underlying principles and processes and you'll be successful for a lifetime.

Many salespeople, for example, have to contend with selling a continuous stream of new products. It's an Information Age challenge. Product life cycles are growing shorter, and companies, to stay competitive, churn out upgrades, new products and new technologies at an accelerating pace. As soon as you master one product or presentation, it becomes obsolete. How do you keep up? Put on the hat of *Master Learner* and learn to learn more quickly and effectively. This book will show you how to do that, equipping you with effective principles, processes and tools to make the task easy. That's the idea. Faced with a new challenge, put on one of the hats: Astute Planner, Trusted Friend, Master Learner, Effective Consultant, Skilled Influencer, or Adept Human Resource Manager.

Imagine you're on the road, making sales calls, and you have six different hats arranged on the back seat of your car. When you put on each hat, you magically gain a distinctly unique set of abilities. You select hats and combinations of them according to the ever-changing circumstances you encounter. Thus, the hats provide you the power to be successful in a limitless number of sales situations. You can get by without them, but the special insights and abilities you gain by using them enable you to accelerate your sales success. That's the idea underlying *The Six Hats for the Constantly Improving Salesperson.*

Each of the hats represents a set of competencies. A competency is an area of activity that is important to your overall success. It's an aspect of your job in which, if you're going to be at all effective, you must gain a certain minimum level of proficiency. If you're going to reach success at a level higher than most, then you must continually improve in each of those aspects of your job.

Let's imagine, for example, that you're a professional basketball player. You understand there are certain aspects of your game in which you must have a minimum level of proficiency. You must be able to dribble, to pass, to shoot, to rebound, to defend, etc. Each of these aspects of the game are competencies. They are shared by everyone in the game, no matter at what level. Your kids playing elementary school basketball can all shoot, dribble, pass, rebound, defend, etc. The difference between them and Michael Jordan is the degree of expertise in each of those competencies.

So it is with you. As a professional salesperson, you need to reach certain minimal levels of expertise in specific aspects of your job, and then you need to continually improve in each of those aspects. Each hat represents one of those essential aspects of your job.

A competency is made up of a combination of principles, processes, and tools. You gain the magic of the hat by first understanding the principle, and then developing your competency in that area by implementing the associated processes. Eventually, as you become proficient in each of the competencies represented by the hats, you develop a set of almost magical abilities. While you can become skilled at a competency, you never become as good as you can be. In the search for continuous personal improvement, there is no finish line.

The key to the power of the six hats is understanding the principles and processes involved in gaining mastery of that aspect of your job.

According to Webster's, a principle is, "a fundamental truth, law, doctrine, or motivating force upon which others are based." If you understand the principles which support each competency, you'll be able to apply that competency to a continuously changing set of circumstances. Many of the Six Hat principles will appear to be common sense observations. And that they may be. I've found that the most powerful sales principles are those that are most easily understood and accepted. The trick, then, is to apply that insight or truth to the salesperson's task.

All of the principles are observations I've made along the way, and refined in the crucible of literally hundreds of sales training sessions with tens of thousands of salespeople around the world. Some of them mark watershed events in my life. In several cases, my discovery of a principle changed the course of my career.

Principles are powerful insights. Don't let the sometimes simplistic nature of them fool you into underestimating their potential effect on your career.

But it's not enough to understand the principles. If it were, all you'd need to be a successful salesperson is a college degree in sales. Knowledge of principles is necessary, but not sufficient. You need some way to apply those principles to the challenges you face. That's where processes come in. Processes unleash the power of your potential by providing you a way to implement the principles.

The dictionary defines process as "a particular method of doing something, generally involving a number of steps or operations." Think of a process as a "how-to." It's the missing link in most sales training, the key that unlocks the power of a principle. Combine a principle with a process, and you'll be powerfully equipped.

For years, I've held a position that is outside the mainstream of most of the motivational speakers, success gurus and sales trainers. Here it is: *Goal setting is overrated!* Don't misunderstand. I believe in goal setting, and it is described as an integral part of one of the hats later in the book. But, as far as being a sure ticket to leading a full and satisfying life, it's overrated. In my experience, every one of the best things I have in my life have come to me, not as a result of setting a goal and working toward it, but rather as a result of adhering to certain principles and processes.

For example, I never set out to find someone to marry. Yet my wife, Coleen, is certainly one of the best things in my life. I met and developed a relationship with her as a result of taking a risk and attending a Parents Without Partners meeting. It was the principle, *It's a good idea to associate with people in the same situation as yourself,* that drove me to seek out a support group. And that led to my meeting her.

Our daughter, Kelly, is certainly one of the best things in my life. Yet we did not set out to adopt an infant. Rather we followed the principle, *it's more blessed to give than to receive*, became foster parents, and eventually opened our home to a child who later became a permanent acquisition to the family.

I could go on and on. My career, my spiritual relationships – every one of the best things I have in my life - came as the result of adhering to principles and implementing processes, not as the result of setting and working at goals. Principles and processes, therefore, are the key to this system.

The third component of a competency is the set of tools you need to use to implement the processes and principles. A tool is anything that you use to help you accomplish your job. Computers, cell phones, sales literature, forms, worksheets, and samples are all examples of tools.

Let's apply these three pieces to the expression, "Give a person a fish, and you feed him for a day, teach him to fish, and you feed him for a lifetime." What does it mean to "teach someone to fish?" It's a matter of principles, processes, and tools.

If you're going to learn to fish, you first need to understand some principles. "Fish eat worms" is a principle. Upon that principle you can build a process. Because "fish eat worms" you can learn to find worms, you can learn to put them on a hook, you can learn to place that hook in the water near where a fish should be. Those are the processes, the "how-to's" that make up the competency of "fishing."

Finally, your efforts to fish will be significantly enhanced if you have effective tools. Everything else being equal, the person with the sharp hooks, strong line, sensitive rod and quality reel will do better than the person with a cane pole and rusty hook. The difference is a function of the tools.

Put together powerful principles, effective processes, and quality tools, and you'll catch fish. It's only when the principle was combined with the process, and enabled by good tools, that the desired result – fish, was obtained. All three pieces, together, make up the competency of "fishing." So, if you want to be a master fisher person, you need to learn the principles, master the processes, and acquire the tools. You'll eat well for the rest of your life.

That's the idea behind the *Six Hats of the Constantly Improving Salesperson.* Understand the principles, learn the processes, use the tools, and you'll be successful for a lifetime. It's a matter of learning to wear six hats.

To help communicate these parts of each hat, we've chosen to add graphic icons. When you see the anchor icon, you'll know that we're discussing a principle. An anchor on a sail boat is that part of the boat that can stabilizes the entire ship and all its occupants, so our principles are the anchors around which you can build your competency.

When you see the arrows icon, you'll know that you're learning a process – a step by step series of actions that show you "how to" turn the principle into an application. These cornerstone principles and processes are the heart of the Six Hats.

When you see the tool icon, you'll know that we're discussing a tool to use in mastering that hat.

Understand these principles and become adept at the processes and comfortable with the tools, and you'll be able to succeed in a countless number of situations, with an unlimited number of people. You'll be equipped to succeed in the Information Age.

The Six Hats

When you think about all the challenges that impact a salesperson's performance, you can categorize them into two basic areas: The need to influence the customer, and the challenge to manage yourself. In the first six months of my first full time outside sales position, I came to realize that my success depended on my ability to do both well. No matter how slick I was in my face-to-face interactions with my customers, if I hadn't organized and motivated myself to be in front of the right customers with the right attitude and fully prepared, it didn't matter. I concluded that I had to become good at both sides of the salesperson's challenge.

The six hats are organized to address those two areas. Illustration #2-1 shows that organization.

THE SALESPERSON'S CHALLENGE

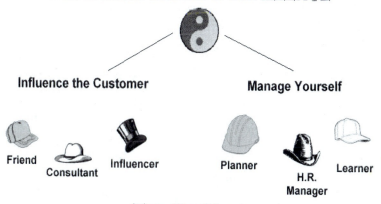

THE SIX HATS

Illustration 2-1

The first hat, *Astute Planner*, bridges the gap between those two major areas of the salesperson's challenge: Working with customers, and managing yourself. In the Information Age, you can't afford to dissipate your time, you must become more effective by mastering the discipline of thinking about what you do before you do it. In other words, planning. This competency describes how to focus on your highest potential customers, to plan for key account strategies, to develop sales call plans, and to organize your time by creating daily, weekly and monthly plans.

The second hat, *Trusted Friend*, describes the competency of creating trusting relationships with customers. In a high tech world full of confusing choices, people (your customers) are hungry for high touch relationships with competent people they can trust. The Information Age demands a more relationship-oriented approach to sales, and this hat provides specific techniques and processes for making good first impressions, finding common ground with almost anyone, understanding and reflecting individual behavior styles, and operating under a strict code of ethics.

The third hat, *Effective Consultant*, focuses on the competency of being seen by your customer as a valuable consultant. This competency is built upon the principles of knowing the customer more effectively than anyone else, and matching the products, programs and services you sell to the deeper needs and interests of the customer. No more features and benefits selling; it's identifying problems and opportunities, and matching them to custom-crafted solutions. When you master this hat, you know how to understand the customer more deeply, more broadly and more specifically, to design your presentations and proposals more effectively, and to leverage every transaction into deeper relationships.

The fourth hat, *Skillful Influencer*, teaches the process approach to selling, and provides specific strategies and tactics for making powerful presentations, closing the sale and handling objections.

The fifth hat, *Adept Human Resource Manager*, describes strategies and techniques for managing your greatest resource: Yourself! Organizing your files, managing information, strategies for time management, overcoming rejection and depression, setting goals -- all these are designed to show you how to wring the most out of your potential.

Finally, the sixth hat, *Master Student,* makes an appeal for lifelong learning and continuous improvement, provides six specific strategies to pursue, and describes our trademarked Menta-Morphosis ™ personal learning system.

Chapter Three:
The First Hat - Astute Planner

📖 It Starts with Information

Most salespeople love to be active — out in our territories, seeing people, solving problems, putting deals together. This activity-orientation is one of the characteristics of a sales personality. A day sitting behind a desk is our idea of purgatory. Unfortunately, this activity orientation is both a strength and weakness. Much of our ability to produce results finds its genesis in our activity orientation. It provides some of the energy to move us to sales success.

But it can be a major obstacle. Far too often, we're guilty of going about our jobs directed by the credo of "Ready, shoot...aim." The luxury of this kind of unfocused activity is a casualty of the Information Age. As a salesperson committed to constant improvement, you understand that, to be effective, you must be focused and thoughtful about everything you do. Activity without forethought and planning is a needless waste of time and energy.

And the most important part of your job to think about is the time you spend in front of your prospects and customers. Of all the different parts of your job, there is nothing more important to think about - nothing more important to plan — than that.

If you were to make a list of everything you do, and then considered each of the items on the list, you'd likely discover that almost everything you do can be done cheaper or better by someone else within your company. Someone else can call for appointments cheaper or better than you. Someone else can check on back orders better than you can. Someone else can fill out a price quote, write a letter, or deliver a sample, cheaper or better than you. In fact, it's likely that the only thing you do that no one else in your company can do cheaper or better than you is interact with your customers. It's the face-to-face interaction with your customers that defines the value you bring to the company. If it weren't for that, your company would have little use for you.

So, the face-to-face interaction with your customer is the core value you bring your company, the reason for your job. Yet, most studies indicate that the average outside salesperson only spends about 25 - 30% of his/her working week actually face-to-face with the customer.

In the light of that, doesn't it make sense to spend some time planning and preparing to make that 30% of your work the highest quality you can possibly make it? Of course it does.

Which brings us to hat number one -- Astute Planner. The salesperson who is devoted to constant improvement puts on the first hat and strives to plan and prepare all the important aspects of the job, investing approximately 20% of the work time planning and preparing for the other 80%.

The Planning Principles

Mastery of this hat is built upon several powerful principles. Here's the first:

Chapter Three: The First Hat - Astute Planner

Good decisions require good information.

It's the Information Age, remember. And that means that, if you're going to be an effective Six Hat Salesperson, you must collect, store, and use good information. You can't make effective plans if the information on which you build those plans is faulty or sketchy.

If you were going to build a home, for example, you'd want to know about the nature of the ground on which the home was to be built. You'd need to have a good idea about what kind of weather conditions the home would be enduring, what the building codes were, what materials were available and what they cost, and what kind of skilled workmen were required. The list could go on and on. The point is that you wouldn't be able to build a home very effectively if you didn't have good information on which to base those plans.

The same principles apply to building a home as well as delivering effective sales performance. In both cases, *good planning requires good information.* It may be that your company provides you all the information you need. But, it's more likely they don't. If you're going to work with good information, you must be the one who collects that information. That means that you must create systems to *collect, store and use* the information that will be most helpful to you. Since our world is constantly producing new information, the system you create isn't something you do once and forget. Rather, it has to be a dynamic system that is constantly processing, storing and using new information.

📖 The Information-Collecting Process

Creating and maintaining your system is a matter of following several specific steps.
Here's the process:

1. Create a list of the categories of information you'd like to have.
2. Working with one category at a time, brainstorm a list of all the pieces of information you'd like to have within that category.
3. Develop a system and some tools to help you collect that information.
4. Store it efficiently.
5. Use it regularly.

Step One. Start by listing the kinds of information you think will be most useful to you.

Think about your job and determine what kinds of information you'd like to have to help you deal effectively with your customers. Here's a partial list that would fit most salespeople:

* Information about your customers and prospects.
* Information about your competitors
*Information about the products, programs and services you sell.

You may have a number of other categories, but this is a basic list with which you can begin.

Step Two. Once you've categorized the kind of information you'd like, you can then think about what information would be ideal to have in each category.

Start at the top and work down. Look at customers and prospects first. What, ideally, would you like to know about them? Some typical pieces of information would include information about the account's total volume of the kind of products you sell, the dates of contracts that are coming up, the people from whom they are currently buying, and so forth. All of that seems pretty basic.

However, most salespeople have no systematic way of collecting and storing that information. So, while you may occasionally ask a certain customer for parts of it, you probably aren't asking every customer for all the information. And, you're probably not collecting it, storing it, and referring to it in a systematic, disciplined way.

Do you think your competitors know exactly how much potential each of their accounts has? Do you think they know other pieces of useful information, like, for example, how many pieces of production equipment each customer has, and the manufacturer and year of purchase of each? Probably not. If you collect good quantitative marketing information, you'll be better equipped to make strategic sales decisions and create effective plans. For example, you'll know exactly who to talk to when the new piece of equipment from ABC manufacturer is finally introduced. And, you'll know who is really ripe for some new cost-saving product that's coming, or the new program your company is putting together.

You may currently be doing a so-so job of collecting information. It's like golf. Anyone can hit a golf ball. But few can do it well. Anyone can get some information. Few salespeople do it well. Doing it well is one indication of mastery of the first hat.

Step Three. Develop a system and some tools.

The single most effective tool is an account profile form. It's an incredibly effective tool that generates and organizes some of the most powerful processes.

Account Profile Form

An account profile form is a form full of questions, or more precisely, spaces for the answers to questions. The questions are all about each of your accounts. The form is the document on which you store that useful information. It can exist in a couple of different forms – paper or electronic. If you're using contact-management software on a laptop computer, then the account profile form can be several screens for each account. If you're not computerized, then it needs to be created on paper. Regardless of the media, the principles and processes are the same.

A well-designed, systematically executed account profile form can be one of your most powerful tools for acquiring a competitive edge. Here's why. First, it provides you a way to collect quantitative information that will allow you to know your customers more thoroughly than your competition. All those pieces of information that you said were potentially important to you can be collected and stored in the blanks on the account profile form. Create a one-page form with blanks in it for each of the quantitative pieces of information you want.

In addition to the quantitative information about the business, you need another version of the form for each of the key individuals within those accounts. That's called a personal profile, and it is your mechanism to collect personal information about the key decision makers. You apply the same concept and principles to the task of collecting personal information about the key decision makers within your accounts. You may end up with one document for the company and 10 to 15 personal profiles for all the key people within that account.

Now, imagine getting ready for the next sales call on that customer and reviewing the things that he likes to talk about, refreshing your memory on the name of his spouse, and the names and schools of each of the kids. As you plan your presentation, you review the primary buying motivation for each of those key people. Do you think you'll be better prepared to have an enjoyable, relationship-building conversation with that customer than your competitor will? Of course you will. Do you think you'll increase your likelihood of delivering a powerful and persuasive presentation? Of course you will.

Finally, the form allows you to store important information someplace other than in your head. The problem with keeping information just in your head is that it isn't always readily accessible. When you want to have a relaxed conversation with one of your customers about his interests, you can't always remember that he golfs and was a starting halfback on his college football team. However, if you have that information stored on a form, you can review it just before you go in to see your customer, and put it uppermost in your mind.

To some degree, every good salesperson implements these concepts. The difference between the run-of-the-mill salesperson and the salesperson who wants to take performance Up-a-Notch, however, is the degree to which the committed salesperson disciplines himself to stick to a systematic approach. Most salespeople do it as they think of it, but don't keep the information systematically. Masters of the Six Hats understand the need to discipline themselves, and thus do a more thorough job of collecting information.

Step Four. Store it efficiently.

You may have done a great job of collecting information, but if you've stored it on old match book covers, coffee-stained post-its, and the backs of old business cards somewhere in the backseat of your car, it's probably not going to do you much good.

If you're computerized, then your computer can be the super tool that allows you to efficiently store the information. If not, you're going to need to create a set of files (yes, manila folders!) in which to store your information. More on this later.

Step Five. Use it regularly.

Before every sales call, review the information you have stored. That review will help you make good decisions about each aspect of the sales call. Likewise, review the information as you create your annual goals and sales plans, when you create account strategies, and when you organize and plan your territories.

As you can tell, an account profile form is a master tool that holds all of this together. If you're going to have any mastery of this hat, you'll need to create this too. In order to help you with this most important task, here's a seven-step process for creating your own account profile form.

Account Profile Process

1. *Identify each of the markets to which you sell.*

You may sell to a number of different kinds of customers. Each different type of business should have it's own version of the form. For example, I sold to hospitals, large outpatient clinics, and independent laboratories. The differences between these institutions were enormous, and each had a different business structure, set of needs, and decision-making apparatus. So each warranted a unique account profile form.

Chapter Three: The First Hat - Astute Planner

2. Create a list.

Begin the form by first listing all of the things you'd like to know about your account. For example, you might find it useful to know the number of employees, the SIC code, which competitors are currently involved in the account, who are your customer's customers, what products they manufacture or what services they offer, and so on. The key is to determine the information that is *useful* to you.

Then, create page two, which is the personal profile. This is the form on which you store information about the individuals within each account. So, you may have one account profile and several personal profiles for the key decision-makers and influencers within the account. List all the things that you'd like to know about each individual decision-maker, influencer, or gatekeeper within that account. This is generally personal information such as where they went to school, their interests and hobbies, who you may know in common, the organizations they belong to, and other similar information. Take several days to develop an exhaustive list, writing down ideas as they come to you.

3. Edit.

Now, edit your list of ideas down to those pieces of information you consider most useful. You probably can't collect everything, so collect the information that is most useful. Start with the basics -- name, title, and so on, and add the important business information -- like how much of each of your product categories that account purchases each year, what kind of business it is, and what are the reporting relationships and decision-making processes.

4. *Design the form.*

Now, create the form with spaces for each of the answers to the questions you listed above. Don't get too involved in creating the perfect looking document. No matter how thorough a job you've done, you'll probably revise the form in a few weeks after you have some experience working with it. So, design something that is workable for now, and let your day-to-day use create the fine-tuning adjustments that you'll make along the way.

If you're working with a computer and a contact-manager program, you may still want to start with a paper form. After you're comfortable that you have all the right pieces of information, you can then incorporate it into the contact manager. This approach may save you hours of frustration later.

5. *Implement.*

Begin to use the form to collect information on every sales call. This doesn't mean that you set down with pen in hand and interrogate every customer, although a little of that is appropriate. You can generally collect the information on the account portion in a formal session. Generally, your customers will be favorably impressed with your professionalism and thoroughness.

That formal approach will not work for the personal portion. With this piece, you'll need to review the form before each sales call, solidifying in your mind the information you already have and determining what you need. Then, in the course of the conversation, attempt to listen specifically for those pieces of information that you're still lacking. Completing the form may take six months of sales calls.

6. Refine.

Review your master form from time to time and revise it as you get experience with it. You'll soon determine what information is impossible to collect, and what really isn't useful. If you're using a computer, wait until this step of the process to load the form into your contact manager.

7. Refer to it.

Store your forms in a place from which you can easily retrieve them each time you call on that account. I suggest you create an account folder for each customer, and that you keep your forms there. Refer to them before every sales call. By reading over the personal information you've stored on the form, you'll find it fresh in your mind, and you'll be much more likely to work it into a conversation. All of your efforts to create the form and collect information will be wasted if you don't use it before every sales call.

Remember, also, to refer to the account information when you're doing your planning. As you know, you can't create good plans without good information. So, the first step in gaining mastery of this hat, astute planner is to create a system to collect, store, and access useful information.

Collecting information about your competitors

Now that you have a system in place to provide good information about your prospects and customers, you need to turn your focus to another area of your business – your competitors. Information about your competitors can be almost as important as that which you collect about your customers. As things change at an increasing rate, it's more important than ever for you to be aware of what your competitors are doing so that you don't get blindsided or seriously outmaneuvered.

That happened to me. To this day, I still get a sick feeling in my stomach as I remember the day when I lost my largest account to my arch competitor. It was an account that made up 20% of my total volume. In my blissful ignorance, I was content to grow my business by calling on the end users and purchasing department, while my competition was successfully building a relationship with the administration. The result? My best account signed a prime vendor, sole-source agreement with my competitor, and within 60 days, I was almost totally out of that account. I was blindsided.

That's a lesson that sticks with me, and one from which you can learn. To become good at knowing what your competition is up to, begin by thinking of yourself a little differently. Here's a simple three-step process for mastering this part of the Astute Planner competency.

Step One. Collect bits and pieces of information

Begin by consciously collecting little bits and pieces of information at every opportunity. For example, you may have lost a bid or a particular piece of business to your competitors. Rather than just moping about it, use it as a learning opportunity. Try to find out from your customer why they awarded the business the way they did. If it was price alone, try to find out how much lower their price was. If it's something else, find out what. That information won't help for that particular piece of business, but it may give you an insight into the pricing policies of your competition. Write the information down on a 3 x 5 card, a piece of scrap paper or a post-it.

Take your good customers to lunch, and casually see if you can steer the conversation in such a way as to learn something about your competition.

Keep your eyes open to the coming and going of competitive salesmen. Note when you see them, and in what account.

Be sensitive and aware of competitive literature, business cards and price quotes lying around. And don't forget to talk with the other salespeople who work for your company to get their insights.

All these are ways to collect bits and pieces of information. By themselves, they won't help much. But, if you combine these bits and pieces, you may very well see trends, uncover strategies, and discover tactics your competition is using.

Step Two. Store the information.

As you collect each bit of information, capture it by writing it down, and putting the note in a manila folder marked "competition." You may even have a separate folder for each major competitor. If you're automated, type the information into your computer, and store it in either a word processing or database file.

Regardless, what you're doing is assembling a quantity of information. Diligently collect those bits and piece of information, and file them away.

Step Three. Use the information.

After you have collected a quantity of these, you'll be able to open that file on a regular basis, consider all the pieces of information, and discover a great deal about your competitors.

The trick is to consistently collect and store information. Eventually you'll assemble an accurate picture. It's like the popular game show "Wheel of Fortune." When Vanna White turns over one letter, it doesn't give you much of a picture of the answer. But after she's turned over several of theses small individual pieces, the whole becomes clear and the answer to the riddle is simple to understand. That's the way collecting information about your competition works.

The back of an old business card on which you noted that you saw a competitive salesperson showing a new line of widgets, by itself, doesn't mean much. But if you filed that along with all the bits and pieces of information you've collected, and then pulled it all out and analyzed it, you might see an entirely different situation. Suppose you reviewed that business card note, and combined it with the note you made to yourself that you saw some sales literature on the competitive widget line on the desk of one of your purchasing agents, and then saw that you lost a major bid to the competition because he quoted a new line at lower that traditional prices. All at once you've uncovered a potential threat to your business. Clearly, your competitor is pushing a new, lower price widget line. You didn't learn that from any one piece of information, but rather from the combination of all those pieces, considered as a whole.

The key to uncovering that information, to discovering what your competition is up to, is to consistently collect pieces of information, store them, and then analyze them as a whole from time to time.

As you may be able to tell, this chapter focuses on skills that previously were not in the toolbox of the typical outside salesperson. But, in the Information Age, much of your ability to make good decisions depends on you being able to collect good information. If you are going to take your performance up-a-notch, you must see yourself as a dealer in information as well as a seller of stuff. The first step in gaining mastery of the Astute Planner hat is to get good at collecting good information.

Chapter Four:
Astute Planner — Part II

Now that you've begun the process of collecting, storing and using good information, you can get serious about planning for your sales success. To do so, you'll need to master some additional principles and processes. Here's the next key principle for mastery of this hat: **You'll always be more effective if you think about what you do before you do it.**

I recall going to see a well-known speaker and author in a two-hour presentation. The auditorium was filled with several hundred people who had paid to learn from this man's insight and wisdom. Early into his presentation, he remarked that he really didn't know what he was going to say, and had not prepared anything, that he would rely on the dynamics of the immediate situation to select his thoughts and words. I grew angry. What arrogance! What followed was something of a disjointed stream-of-consciousness monologue that prompted most in the audience to go away having learned nothing.

If that speaker had gathered some information about the size and demographics of the audience, if he had organized his presentation in an easily-understood format, if he had prepared handouts to visually support his verbal presentation, if he had searched his memory for examples and illustrations that would have resonated with this audience, if he had spent some time meeting individuals before the presentation, if he had telephone interviewed some of the audience before the meeting -- if he had done any or all of these things, his presentation would have been far more effective.

That's an easy conclusion for us to reach. Of course he would have been far more effective, of course his audience would have gained much more, of course he would have influenced some people to want to hear him again – if he had taken the time to prepare the presentation.

Of course, it's always more effective to think about what you do before you do it. Can you imagine a football team not creating a game plan or not practicing before the big game? Can you imagine a musician not preparing a piece of music before the recital? Can you imagine a politician not practicing the big speech? Or a doctor not reviewing the xrays and the procedure prior to a major surgery? Or a lawyer barging into a case without having planned it? The answer to all these questions is, "Of course not." In every event of any importance at all, professional, effective human beings plan and prepare beforehand. It's an essential step toward success.

The same is true for salespeople. If we think about what we do before we do it, providing we think about it in the right way, we'll significantly improve our performance. Unfortunately, many salespeople are often guilty of the same mindset that provided this speaker an excuse for his lack of concern and preparation. Our intuition and incredible spur-of-the-moment, ad-lib skills will get us by. WRONG!

You have a great treasury of wisdom and insight that you've acquired through a rich set of life experiences. Much of that wisdom and insight can be directly applied to your sales job, if you will only tap into it and use it. Of course you'll be able to tap into some of that accumulated expertise on the spur of the moment, but you'll be far more effective if you take the time to tap into it before you get into the situation.

If you're going to be effective with this hat, you'll think about what you do before you do it – you'll think about every telephone call, every sales call, every customer, every presentation, every interaction with your customers and prospects. Yet it's not enough to think about what you do before you do it, you must also think about things in the right way. The next section shows you how to do it.

 Good planning is a matter of asking yourself the right questions, and then answering them with detail and precision.

An amazing thing happens when you ask yourself questions – you think of the answers! What sounds so elementary is really a powerful key to unlocking your success. When you ask yourself a good question you stimulate your thinking. For example, you could ask yourself, "What are the three most effective things I could do to improve my sales performance?" That question would prompt you to analyze your performance, develop some possible changes in your behavior, and then select three that appear to be the highest priority. That's a very worthwhile set of thoughts. And they were prompted by the question you asked yourself.

While this is just one example, the principle is incredibly powerful. Learn to ask yourself good questions, and you'll think more effectively.

It follows, then, that if you want to think well, you need to ask yourself the best questions. For example, you could ask yourself the question, "What are all the things that the customer will not like about me in this upcoming sales call?" Ask that question, and your mind will dredge up all the flaws and faults you've filed away in your memory. That's probably not the most effective way to prepare for a sales call. After thinking about that question, you're liable to be depressed and discouraged. Rather, you could ask yourself the question, "What are two or three things I could find out about the customer that would uncover things we have in common?" Think about the answer to that question, and your mind will dwell on your customer, not yourself, and focus on finding common ground in order to build a relationship. Which of those two questions will be the better one for you to ask yourself prior to a sales call?

The answer is obvious. But the point is this – if you're going to adequately prepare and plan for your sales interchanges, you need to ask yourself the right questions. When you ask yourself the right questions, you think in the most effective way.

In order to implement this principle, you'll need to master two basic processes. Each of these processes is really a series of questions, asked in a certain sequence. Master these two processes, and you'll master the first hat, Astute Planner. You'll gain a competency that will serve you well the rest of your working life.

The Processes

To implement this principle and acquire the power of the first hat, you'll need to master two processes: The prioritization process, and the planning process.

The prioritization process is used to help you make good decisions about where to spend your time, about what to plan. There is just not enough time in the day for you to plan everything. So, you must first prioritize those things that are important enough to plan. You then follow that up with the planning processes. You'll find that you use the two together.

📖 The Prioritization Process:

This is a four-step process that you can use over and over from now until you retire.
1. Select the category to be prioritized.
2. Identify the outcome.
3. Create criteria.
4. Apply those criteria.

Let's apply those four steps to an example.

Step One. Select the category to be prioritized. Ask yourself, "Of all of these (what ever you're considering) which is the most important?"

There are a number of areas that you may want to prioritize - each of which are separate aspects of your job. For example, if you sell a wide variety of products, you could prioritize those products in order to select those that have the highest priority for you to pursue. If you have 20 things to do tomorrow, you'd certainly want to prioritize those. As an example, we're going to work with an area that may be the single most important category of your job — your customers.

So, step one is easy and relatively simple - select the category to be prioritized. In our example, we're going to select the category of "customers."

Step Two. Identify the outcome you want. Ask yourself, "What should be the end result of this process?"

In other words, with what do you want to end up? In this case, let's say that you want to end up with a set of three categories of customers - A's, B's, and C's. Let's further say that you want your A's to be the highest potential account, representing the top 5 – 20% of your accounts. You want the B category to contain the middle 30 – 50% of all your accounts, and the C's to be the lowest potential 30 – 50 % of your accounts. You've identified where you want to end up.

Step Three. Create criteria. Ask yourself, "On what basis should I make that determination?"

A "criterion" is something by which you judge something else. It's a standard or benchmark by which you measure that thing with which you're working.

In this case, we start out by remembering that we're working on our customers, and keeping in mind that we want to end up with three classes of customers. So, we've got to develop some criteria to use to separate those customers into the three categories. I'd suggest we think in terms of "potential."

Normally, when I ask salespeople to identify their A, B or C accounts, they'll pull out a sales report, and show me who purchased the most. But that's history, not potential. I'm interested in the future, not the past. So, I suggest that we focus on future potential. That means that we've got to determine which customers have the highest potential, and which have degrees of lesser potential.

What constitutes "high potential?" From a salesperson's perspective, high potential is the ratio between the likelihood of sales dollars (or income dollars) being generated in return for time invested. You may have a potentially huge account, for example, but because of some of the philosophy or history at that account, you'd have to invest years to begin to receive any sales dollars in return. That would not be a high potential account, because of the out of balance relationship between potential sales dollars to

Chapter Four: Astute Planner – Part II

your investment of time. A more likely prospect could be a customer with smaller volume, but who could be converted relatively easily. In that case, the ratio between sales dollars and time invested would be more in your favor.

When you determine high potential, use two criteria. The first is *quantified potential*. Quantified potential refers to the total dollars available in that account. In other words, how much of your product can they buy? Obviously each account has a potential to purchase differing amounts of your product. If you can collect that information accurately and with detail, you'll have a good sense of that account's quantified potential. That's the objective criterion.

But that's only half of the issue. The second criterion is subjective. I call it potential *partnerability*. *Partnerability* is that subjective feeling you gain about the account's potential to eventually becoming a partner – a loyal, committed, deeply engaged customer who buys everything they can from you, respects you, and looks out for your best interest. This criterion takes into account the chemistry between the two companies and between yourself and your customers, the philosophy of the account, the fit between their needs and your offerings, etc. Is the account just a price buyer, or is it open to creative proposals from you? Is it a progressive, growing organization? Those are the issues that comprise *partnerability*. You may have one account that has huge quantifiable potential, but because of the philosophy or personalities of the decision makers, no foreseeable *partnerability*. That account would not be a high-potential account.

➤ Step Four. Apply the criteria. Ask yourself, "What happens when I apply the criteria?"

You could apply the criteria, in our example, this way. On a sheet of paper, create three columns. In the first, list all of your customers and prospects. Then, in the second, give each of them a 1 - 100 rating on their "quantified potential." Give a 100 to the account in your territory that could purchase the most of your products or services. Assign a one to the smallest.

After you've rated all of your customers and prospects on "quantified potential," move on to the third column. In this one, use the same 1- 100 rating, but this time rate each customer's "potential partnerability." A one hundred in partnerability indicates an account where all the subjective factors are in your favor. A one is a customer in which none of them are favorable.

Now, add the second and third columns. The sum of those two criteria will give you a number which you can use to sort each of your customers into A, B and C categories. Call the top rated 5 to 20 percent of all your prospects and customers A accounts. So, if you have 20 total customers, you should identify 1 to 4 as "A" customers. Remember, these represent the highest potential dollars returned for time invested.

Then, cull out those who appear to offer a minimal return on time invested. Take somewhere between 10 to 60 percent and put them in the "C" column. Those are your lowest priority prospects and customers.

Finally, put all those who are left over in the "B" column. They represent the middle group of prospects and customers.

You've just worked through the prioritization process. In so doing, you've prioritized the most salient aspect of your business – your prospects and customers.

Congratulations! Now, you can use that process to prioritize other aspects of your business. Use it to prioritize your prospects, your products, your sales calls, etc. Remember the first principle, *You'll always be more effective if you think about what you do before you do it.* Thinking about where to apply your time most effectively by prioritizing the most important aspects of your job is one of the best things you can do. Put on the first hat, and prioritize every important aspect of your job. Then, you'll be ready to master the next discipline of the first hat, you'll be ready to plan effectively.

The Planning Process

The planning process is a matter of asking a set of seven questions of yourself, asking them in the right sequence, and then answering them in writing. The resulting written answers become your plan. You can use this process to plan anything worth planning – your territory, your approach to key accounts, each sales call, your month, your week, etc.

Here is each step and the seven questions to ask.

 Step One. Start with a goal. Ask, "What's the objective?"

Always, the first step in the creation of a plan is the identification of the purpose of the plan. If there is no purpose, why have a plan? The purpose of the plan is your objective. Regardless of what aspect of your business you're working on – planning a sales call, developing a strategy for a key account, organizing your territory, creating a plan for a new product line -- you must begin with an answer to this question.

In order to illustrate each of the steps of this process, we'll identify a situation and then work through it step by step. Let's begin by setting a personal, financial goal. While sales is a fulfilling, challenging career, most of us wouldn't be doing it if we didn't get paid. To some extent, our sales success is a means to an end, not an end in itself. And that end is our financial rewards. So, let's focus on your personal financial goals. Let's say you're going to select an objective with which to begin the planning process, and that objective is, "To make $75,000 in the next calendar year."

Step Two. Assess the situation. Ask, "What's the situation?"

This step requires you to describe, as accurately as possible, the current situation as it relates to the area about which you're thinking.

Let's consider our objective from above. You've decided you want to make $75,000 next year. So, you describe the salient aspects of your current financial situation like this:

You have a salary of $50,000. You're paid a commission of ten percent of all sales above your quota. Last year you had a quota of $750,000 and just made it. This year your quota is $850,000. To achieve your goal, you'll need to do considerably better than last year.

You've just described your situation.

Step Three. Identify the obstacles. Ask, "What will hinder me from achieving the goal?"

Identifying obstacles is a powerful step in the planning process. This step alone will give you incredible confidence and positive power to achieve your goal. As always, you just think the question in as much detail and precision as possible. The resulting answers to the question form the next step in the planning process.

In the example, let's say that you have identified these obstacles:
- Only three of your current accounts are growing.
- Two new competitors are active in your territory.
- There are a lot of changes going on in your market.

Step Four. Identify your strengths and your resources. Ask "What do I have available to me that I can use to accomplish my goal?"

Soberly consider your strengths and your resources. What do you have on your side. Do you have some personal skills that you can apply? Has your company provided you some helpful tools, strategies, or competitive advantages? Is there something working in your favor?

In our example, let's say that you may have a hot new product line, a commitment on the part of your credit department to loosen the rules a bit and speed up the credit-approval process, and you have your bosses' verbal assurances that she'll do everything in her power to help you penetrate those large accounts.

Step Five. Create an overall plan. Ask, "How am I going to accomplish my objective?"

This is the heart of the process. Now, you must consider the best way to reach your goal, taking into consideration the current state of affairs, the obstacles you must face, and your strengths and assets.

In our example, let's say you write the following plan.
1. *Focus my time on high-potential accounts, expanding the business in "A" accounts by 50%.*

a. Get the boss to negotiate with the corporate office for some favorable terms and concessions.
   b. Push the new product line aggressively.
2. Acquire five new accounts.
   a. Use the new product line as a door opener.
   b. Get the credit department to approve some of the formerly marginal customers who may be having a difficult time buying from my competitor.

Step Six. Identify the materials and tools you'll need. Ask, "What will I need?"

In this step, identify all the tools and materials you'll need. In our example, for instance, you might say that you need:

1. Some forms to help identify the highest potential accounts.
2. A list of high-potential prospects.
3. All the usual sales aids.
4. A bunch of new credit apps
5. Some literature and samples of the new line.

Step Seven. Create a detailed action plan. Ask "Specifically, what steps should I take?"

This requires you to think very specifically, and to create a to-do list that precisely identifies each of the steps you'll need to follow, to put them in sequence, and to assign a deadline completion date to each.

In our example, we've arrived at a skeleton plan for the first half of our overall plan. Although the final plan would be more detailed than this, the example below is designed to simply illustrate the process:

1. Focus my time on high-potential accounts, expanding the business in "A" accounts by 50%.
    a. Identify who those are.
        1. Collect some good information using an account profile form. Jan.15
        2. Discuss the results with the boss. Feb. 3.
        3. Agree on the top 20% Feb. 1
    b. Get the boss to negotiate with corporate for some favorable terms and concessions. Feb 15
    c. Push the new product line aggressively.
        1. Make appointments to collect info in each of them. Feb 15
        2. Have initial presentations made in each. March 15
        3. Push forward on demonstrations /evaluations as appropriate.

When you've finished this simple seven-step planning process, you will have created the best plan you're capable of developing. You now have in place a specific strategy for accomplishing your goal, along with a checklist of tasks and dates by which to measure your progress. You created that plan by following the seven-step planning process, asking yourself the questions and answering them in writing. The planning process will work for any aspect of your job. Discipline yourself to use this process, and you'll be well on your way to becoming a master of the first hat.

In order to show you how to apply this process to other aspects of your job, we're going to focus on some powerful applications below.

Applying the Planning Process to "A" Accounts.

You can, and should, apply the seven-step strategy development process to every one of your "A" accounts at least once every three months, but preferably, every month. In so doing, you will create a plan for the most effective things you can do.

Here's an illustration of how to apply the smart planning process to create a strategy for an "A" account.

Step One. What's your objective?

I know you want to sell stuff. But that's too general. In the next six months, what specifically would you like to accomplish with this account? Is it to meet two or three of the key decision makers? To successfully introduce a new line? To increase your commodity business by 10 percent? To increase your gross margins by a point or two? Got the idea? Be specific.

Step Two. What's the situation?

This question requires you to outline the big picture of the account. What's happening within the organization? What role does your company play? What is this customer trying to do? What changes have occurred recently? What competitors are active with this account?

Step Three. What are the obstacles?

Specifically, what's stopping you? Is it a well-entrenched competitor? If so, who is it? And to what degree does he have the business? Or is it a less than favorable purchasing agent or department head? Or maybe a philosophy that exists in the organization? The more detailed and specific you can be with your obstacle analysis, the easier it is to create an effective strategy.

Step Four. What strengths/resources do you have to help you accomplish that?

You may have a great relationship with one of the decision makers, or you may have one or two products already in the account, etc. Look at it realistically. Do you have anything going for you?

Step Five. How are you going to achieve your objective?

This question requires you to outline your basic strategy. Are you going to low-bid the next project? Are you going to take the purchasing agent out to a ball game? What is your basic strategy for achieving your goal?

Step Six. What do you need?

This question asks what materials, literature, help and support you need. Do you need a letter, a copy of an article, some samples, the assistance of a product specialist, the boss's help, etc? What are the things you're going to need to use to help you accomplish your action plan?

Step Seven. What specific steps do you need to take to accomplish that?

If you're going to meet the corporate executives, you may want to:
* *Get their names from the receptionist.*
* *Ask Bill, your contact, to call them and set up and appointment.*
* *Fax a short introductory note to them, then follow up with a phone call asking for an appointment.*
* *When you get the appointment, collect some information to use to present the "systems" proposal.*
* *Bring Jack, the sales manager, on the second appointment.*

Notice that this is a specific list of exactly what you need to do in order to accomplish the objective you described.

Discipline yourself to ask -- and answer -- these questions, in this order, for each of your "A" accounts. You'll take a giant step forward in working smart.

📖 Planning Your Month, Week, and Day

Let's say that you've taken the couple hours at the beginning of the month to work through plans for each of your high-potential accounts. You've got a stack of twenty pages. What now?

Consolidate all of those decisions into a monthly, weekly and daily plan. Review your lists of "steps to take," and lay them out as to when in the month you want to accomplish each. That's a skeletal monthly plan. Then break that down to weekly plans for each week. Finally, at the end of each day, review what you actually did accomplish, add in any new important issues, and create a plan for the next day.

Planning for sales calls

Here's yet one more, vitally important place to exercise your new competency of the first hat. All of the previous planning exists to bring you to this point – where you are thinking about the most effective things you can do with your customers. Let's call that 'planning a sales call.' The process of planning a sales call is the same as with the other planning. It's just a little less intense – think of it as an abbreviated version of the basic planning process. Ask yourself these questions, and use an index card or computer to capture your bulleted responses.

Chapter Four: Astute Planner – Part II

Step One. What do you want to accomplish?

A plan for a sales call, like any other plan, always begins with an objective. Without it, why make the call? If you set out to accomplish nothing, you'll probably be successful.

Step Two. What's the situation?

Note just a few words summarizing the situation as you best understand it. The process of putting words in writing will help you think with detail and precision. The more precise your thinking, the more accurate and effective your plans.

Step Three. What agreement do you want to end up with?

I believe that every sales call should end in some agreement between you and your customer. If nothing else, you can agree to visit again. The clearer you define the agreement you want to end up with, the more likely it is that you'll actually do so.

Step Four. How are you going to do that?

Here are the action steps. Just what exactly are you going to do, in what sequence?

Step Five. What do you need to do that?

Answer this question by gathering the materials, notes and information you'll need to accomplish your plan.

I've timed this process for myself and thousands of salespeople in my seminars. It takes an average of two minutes to plan a sales call, if you've done all the other work. Those two minutes spent thinking about a sales call will dramatically increase the effectiveness of that call.

Do this, and you'll stay focused on the most effective things you can do with your time. You'll become a master of the first hat – Astute Planner.

📖 Trying on the First Hat

OK, so how do you actually fold these principles, processes and tools into your daily routine? First, let's review the three principles we discussed:

1. Good decisions require good information.
2. You'll always be more effective if you think about what you do before you do it.
3. Good planning is a matter of asking yourself the right questions, and then answering them with detail and precision.

We articulated these processes to help you implement the principles:

* information-collecting
* account profile
* competitor information
* prioritization
* planning

So, where to begin? Start with information. If your company has an account profile tool, begin to use it with more detail and diligence. If it doesn't, then immediately begin to develop your own version, or discuss it with your sales manager. You can begin to rough draft your form in an hour or two. So why not do it tonight? And begin to experiment with using it tomorrow. That's a good start.

As long as you're thinking about information, in the next few days, label a manila folder with the word "competitors," and put it on the front seat of your car, where you'll notice it from time to time. That will remind you to be collecting those bits and pieces of information and storing them in the file.

One more thing you can do almost immediately. Start planning every sales call by using the planning process.

Those three activities will get you quickly into this hat, with a minimum of hard work and a great likelihood of seeing immediate results. Spend a couple of weeks ironing out the details, and turning those behaviors into habits.

When you've collected sufficient information, you'll be ready to move to the prioritization and planning processes. You really need to set aside a full day or two in a mini-retreat in order to focus your time and attention on accomplishing those tasks. Once you get on the other side of that project, you'll find yourself working far more effectively. Not harder, smarter.

Which shouldn't surprise you. After all, you're now wearing the first hat, Astute Planner.

Wearing the Hat

When you've fully mastered the principles, processes and tools associated with the first hat, you'll be operating with forethought in all the important aspects of your job.

You'll be systematically and continuously collecting good information about your customers and your competitors. It won't be an isolated event, it will be a regular part of your every day routine. Every sales call you make will be an opportunity to learn more about your customers.

Every year, at least once a year, you'll set aside a day or two for a planning retreat. At that, you'll create goals and plans for the year. You'll review all your accounts and prospects, prioritizing them into ABC categories. You'll develop annual strategic plans for your key accounts.

Every quarter, you'll set aside time to review your progress and make fine-tuning adjustments. You'll think carefully about each of your A accounts, and refine your strategic plans for them. You'll review the information in your competitor file, and garner from that an understanding of your competitor's strategic and tactics.

Every month, you'll create written plans for each of your "A" accounts, and consolidate those action steps into an overall plan for the month.

Every week, you'll create plans for the most effective use of your week.

At the end of each day, you'll plan the next. You'll think about every sales call and every customer contact, and create a plan for each of them.

And, as a result of wearing this hat, you'll become far more effective and rise to the top in your career.

Chapter Five:

Using the Six Hats to Take Your Performance Up-A-Notch

Challenge: My customers don't have much time to spend with me.

Your customers used to be able to spend more time with you. But lately, it seems like they are on tighter schedules and are harder to see. You just can't spend as much time with them as you'd like, because they're pressuring you to move on.

This is a real information-age issue. You know how confused and pressured you feel these days. Your customers feel the same way. As pressures brought on by rapid change, growing competition and the need for every organization to become more streamlined and efficient have hit your customers, their organizations have reacted by trying to make their employees more productive. As a result, your customers have too much to do and not enough time in which to do it, just like you. Some of your customers are walking around with day-planners under their arms today, when, just a couple of years ago, they didn't know what one was. Time, more so than money, is the precious currency of the Information Age.

It's not that your customers don't like you, (although they may not) nor that they are not interested in your products and services. It's just that they have too much to do, and simply don't have as much time to spend with you as you'd like.

Implications...

This development is truly ominous because the implications strike to the heart of your ability to perform for your company. Let's think for a minute about the value you bring your company. Why do they employ you? What do they really need you and other salespeople to do? If you were to boil it down to its most fundamental level, you'd probably say that your company needs you to create relationships and spend face-to-face time with your customers.

Anything that interferes with your ability to spend face-to-face, person-to-person time with your customer threatens the heart of your job, the core of the value you bring your company.

That's what makes this challenge ominous. If you can't spend quality time in front of the customer, your days as a salesperson are numbered.

Applying the Six Hats...

First, put on the second hat, *Trusted Friend*. Remember to respect your customers' time constraints. If you try to overstay your welcome, you'll only succeed in making him/her more irritated with you. Do unto him as he would have you do unto him. Protect the relationship.

Then, put on the first hat, *Astute Planner*. Focus on making the time that you do have with him more productive for both of you. Think of the issue being *quality* time, not *quantity time*. Here are three strategies that will work for you.

Chapter Five: Using the Six Hats to Take Your Performance Up-A-Notch

★ 1. Focus on the quality of the time you have with your customer.

If you're not going to have as much time in front of the customer as you'd like, then you must concentrate on making the time that you do have as valuable and productive as possible. That requires you to spend more time planning and preparing for each sales call.

Gone are the days when you could just "stop in." Rather, make sure that you have at least three things prepared for every sales call:

* a specific objective -- what do you want to accomplish in this call?
* an outline of how you're going to accomplish that objective, and
* all the necessary tools you'll need to do it.

Use the planning process to make sure that you're spending high quality time with your customer. That way, the actual time that you spend with your customers will be more productive. Your customer will appreciate your organization and your respect of his time, too.

★ 2. Set an agenda – talk in terms of the customer's needs.

Begin every sales call with an agenda. Tell your customer what you want to cover and how you're going to proceed. Mention the needs and objectives in which he is interested, and explain how you're going to address them. This will relieve him of the worry that you're going to appropriate his time unnecessarily, and will allow him to focus on you.

For example, at the beginning of your sales call, you could say something like this:

"John I know you're interested in the cost payback of a possible investment in a new telephone system. I'd like to share

with you some of the numbers that others have used to investigate this kind of purchase. After we go through these, I'll address any other questions you may have, and then we'll talk about the next step in this process. Does that sound reasonable?"

 3. Always have something of value to discuss.

This is more of a longer-range strategy. As you consistently hold to this principle, over time you'll build up a certain expectation in the customer's mind. Don't expect an immediate payback from this strategy, but, nonetheless, stick to it for the long hall.

Think of the time that your customer does spend with you as an investment by the customer. Put yourself in his shoes, and see the situation from his perspective. Is he gaining something of value from you in exchange for his investment of time? You want the answer to that question to be "Yes."

In order to generate that perception in your customer's mind, make sure that every time you see him, you have something of value to share or to discuss with him. That means something in which the customer is interested. If you have nothing the customer will think is of value, don't take his time. Wait until you do have something to see him.

After a few such calls, your customer will come to respect you and look forward to your calls, knowing that you're not there just to work some agenda of yours, but rather he'll come to expect to gain something from your sales calls.

You'll find it easier to make appointments and get time with your customers when you've built in them the expectation that the time spent with you will be well worth the cost of it.

Chapter Six:
The Second Hat - Trusted Friend

A couple of years ago I decided to hire a lawn care company to fertilize my lawn. My next door neighbor had been using that company for a couple of years, and his lawn looked significantly better than mine. So I got the name and phone number of the company, and called them.

When I spoke to the salesman, I explained my situation, and asked him what kind of deals they offered. He told me they would come out and treat my lawn for an introductory price, and then leave a bill in a plastic envelope hanging from my door. I said OK, and asked them to leave a written description of their service and options, so that I could review it and then decided what program to sign up for. He said they would, and that I could then cancel anytime I wanted.

All at once, my ears perked up and I grew suspicious. First, he said he'd leave me the information for me to review, and now he was saying that I could cancel anytime I wanted.

"What do you mean?" I asked.

"We'll start you next week, and you can cancel anytime you want."

I said "Wait a minute, you said you'd leave some literature, and now you're saying that I can cancel anytime. I'm not committing for the summer, I just want to review my options and then make a choice."

He said, "But…"

I said, "That's not how I want to do this."
He said, "But,"
And I said, "No!" and hung up.

Let's analyze what happened. I was as ready a buyer as there could be. I knew the company, and I had already decided to buy. It should have been a simple, easy transaction. But the salesperson said something that made me suspicious of him. First, he said that they would leave the information for me in an envelope. Then he said that I could cancel at anytime, implying that my decision to have them come out the first time was a commitment for a season-long program. That may have been a very reasonable offer, but I saw it as a contradiction. First he told me one thing, and then he told me something that contradicted that. I got a suspicious feeling about the salesperson. I decided that I couldn't trust him. And since I couldn't trust him, I couldn't trust the company.

I knew the company was competent, the service was adequate, the price was fair, and I wanted to buy. What happened? I lost trust in the salesperson. And that was reason enough not to buy. The reason the salesperson didn't make the sale had nothing to do with the classic things on which we salespeople like to focus. Rather, it had to do with my feelings about him.

The point of the story? In our rapidly changing world, where it is more and more difficult to distinguish your product and your company from the competition, the role of the relationship between you, the salesperson, and your customer is more important than ever before.

If you're going to be an effective salesperson in the Information Age, you must be competent at building relationships with a variety of different kinds of people – your customers. You've got to be able to cause your customers to see you as a competent person they can trust, someone with whom they are comfortable. If you are going to take your performance up-a-notch, you must become a master of the second hat: Trusted Friend.

That doesn't mean that you have to make friends of your customers in the traditional sense of the word, although you may very well do so. But what it does mean is that you understand three aspects of friendship. Friends are *comfortable* with one another, friends *trust* each other, and friends *respect* each other. Then, you work, with science and discipline, to get very good at influencing your customers *to trust you, to respect you,* and *to be comfortable* with you. Regardless if you see your customers for only a few moments, or whether you visit them regularly over the years, you can still apply the principles and processes of the second hat.

Learning to use the second hat in every sales interaction will provide you a powerful competitive advantage. In spite of the Internet, fax machines, email, mail-house catalogues, telemarketers, pagers and cell phones, the role of the personal, one-on-one relationship in sales will grow in importance, not shrink. Certainly there will be buyers who prefer the impersonal world of the Internet, or who don't mind the inconvenience and time lost by shopping at the big boxes. But, more and more, the mature decision-maker will come to rely on a relationship with someone who he/she knows and trusts to guide his buying decisions.

Why is that? Because of Shredded Wheat! Remember my experience in the grocery store? When faced with a confusing array of choices, too much to do and too little time in which to do it, I resorted to a relationship with a brand I knew and trusted. It was the relationship upon which I relied.

A natural reaction to a high tech world is to seek out high touch relationships. The knee-jerk reaction to a situation of overwhelming confusion and uncertainty is to lean on a relationship with a competent person you know and trust. Your customers, as their worlds become more and more turbulent, will seek out trusting relationships. The salesperson who can make the customer feel comfortable, who can be seen as a competent person the customer can trust, will gain an advantage. You achieve that position by developing high-touch relationships – turning your customers into friends.

Being seen as competent and trustworthy -- a friend -- is a competency. Welcome to the second hat – becoming a Trusted Friend. It's based on an incredibly powerful principle: **People find reasons to buy from people they trust, and with whom they are comfortable and confident.**

Look at buying from the perspective of the buyer. There are two issues that override almost every other consideration: Time and risk. Just a few years, your customers had more time to invest in the buying decision than they do today. In the Information Age, time is one of the most precious commodities. It matters little whether your buyers are individual consumers making major purchases, like autos or expensive new suits, or whether they are making a major capital investment decision on behalf of their organization. They have less time today to give to that decision.

The natural reaction to a situation where you have too little time to devote to a buying decision is to fall back on a relationship with someone (or some company) you know and trust. Remember my Shredded Wheat decision? I could

Chapter Six: The Second Hat – Trusted Friend

have read every label, looking for the best nutritional combination, or I could have upholstered my calculator and worked out the best value in terms of ounces per cents, or I could have just taken the cheapest product on the shelf. But I did none of those. Faced with too many things to look at and not enough time, I resorted to a relationship with a brand that I knew and trusted, something with which I was comfortable.

"But a brand isn't a person," you're thinking. That's right, but the principle is the same. It's the relationship that saves you time, no matter if that relationship is with a brand, a company, or a person.

As I'm writing this, I'm preparing to buy a car. I've already decided that I'm going to limit my search to one of the dealers on the main thoroughfare closest to my house. Why? Because I don't want to take the time to drive all over town. Within a three mile radius of my house is a Toyota dealer, as well as Ford, Chevrolet, Dodge, Mercury, and Volkswagen dealers. Is there really anything to be gained by looking at all the other brands? Are they really that much different? Probably not. Isn't shopping all the available brands going to be a waste of time? I think so.

And here's an even greater heresy for the automobile executives – I really don't have a preference for a brand. We're going to buy a mid-size sedan. Looked at objectively, is there really much of a difference between a Camry and a Taurus? Or between the offerings of all of those other brands? From my perspective, the features are all about the same and the price is about the same. Competitive pressures have meant that no one model can get significantly ahead of the other, and no one can price their products too far away from the other's price. Sound familiar?

Frankly, we'll probably buy from the first salesperson who impresses us as honest, competent, and concerned about our best interests.

Our perspective isn't that unusual. In the overwhelmingly competitive Information Age economies, time is a critical component. And relationship, as evidenced by our perception of the salesperson as competent, confident and trustworthy, saves us time.

Risk is another of the two primary issues influencing us to rely on a trustworthy, competent salesperson. It's my belief that, for most buyers, risk is the ultimate deciding factor. It's not the cost, in financial terms, of a decision, it's the risk. I define risk as the social, psychological, emotional and financial cost customers must incur if they make a mistake.

Here's an illustration to help you understand this concept. Imagine that your spouse has asked you to pick up a package of disposable cups on the way home from work today because you're having friends over for dessert and drinks tonight. You stop at the local grocery store, and make a selection between brand A and brand B. You pick brand A.

When you bring them home, your spouse mixes up a pitcher of margaritas and pours one. The drink leaks out of the bottom of the cup and puddles on the counter. There is a hole in the bottom of the cup. You pour your drink into another cup and it leaks, too. In fact, every one of the cups you bought is defective.

What happens to you in this instant in time? What is the consequence of your decision? I don't know about you, but I would be the recipient of some negative emotion. My spouse would be upset at me. That may be the most painful cost of your decision. But there are other costs.

Chapter Six: The Second Hat - Trusted Friend

You're going to have to fix the problem. If there's time, you'll have to run back to the store and replace the cups. So, in addition to the emotional cost, you must pay in terms of extra time and additional money. All because of your bad decision. You accepted that risk when you made your decision.

Here's a simple exercise to help you understand this concept. Draw a short vertical line. At the top of the line write the number 25. At the bottom, write the number zero. Now on a scale of 0 - 25, where would you put the risk of buying a package of disposable cups? It's close to zero.

Here's an example at the other end of the scale. I have an adoption agency as a client. When a young lady is in a crisis pregnancy, and she's making a decision as to whether or not to release her unborn child for adoption, how big a risk is that for her? Most people say that it's a 25. It's a lifetime of consequences for at least four people. That's a very high risk.

The point of this exercise is to see the situation from your customer's point of view. When you ask your prospects to say yes to you, they are accepting some risk. Each decision you ask of them carries with it a different degree of risk. Setting an appointment with you is one level of risk, taking the time to trial your product is another, while committing to a multi-year contract is another, greater risk.

Imagine a typical prospect. Then think of the typical offer or decision you ask of that person. Now, put yourself in his shoes, and see the situation through his eyes. On the 0 - 25 scale, how much risk does he accept when he says "yes" to you?

Here's an easy way of calculating it. Just ask yourself what happens to that individual if you, or your company, messes up. If you don't show up for the appointment, or turn out to be a real jerk, your customer has only lost 30 minutes or so. Not a great risk. If the trial of your product turns out to be a failure, you've cost your customer some time and money as well as some time and inconvenience of the other people involved. That's a greater risk. But what about the multi-year contract? If your company doesn't fulfill your end of the deal, your customer could lose his job!

You now have an idea of how your customer looks at the buying decision. The greater the risk, the more difficult the decision.

At this point, you're probably thinking, "OK, so how can I reduce the risk for my customers?"

You know the answer. Build a relationship. Make a friend. Cause your customer to see you as a competent person he can trust, as someone with whom he is comfortable. Relationship mitigates risk. The greater the relationship, the more the customer is comfortable with you, the more he trusts you, the more confident he is in you, the less is the perceived risk. And so, we've discovered a powerful selling principle: **Relationships save the customer time and mitigate the risk.**

Are you convinced? Good, then let's look at each of these three aspects of friendship: comfort, trust, and respect, and apply the principles and processes of the second hat. Let's look at the issue of "comfortable" first. Here's the guiding principle: **People are most comfortable with people who are like themselves.**

This is such an obvious principle that I'm hesitant to include it. Of course, we understand that people are comfortable with people who are like themselves. That's why your friends are people who are your age, with your values, and your interests. It's why people who are of the same economic and social status live near one another,

Chapter Six: The Second Hat – Trusted Friend

belong to the same organizations, and attend the same churches.

The problem is not that we don't understand this principle, it's that we don't apply it to our sales careers. Let's think about this a minute. If people buy from people with whom they are comfortable, and if people are comfortable with people like themselves, and if we work with all kinds of people – our customers -- then shouldn't we.....*be like our customers?*

Shouldn't we, to the degree that we are able, influence our customers to be comfortable with us by being like our customers? Whose responsibility is it to make the sale, anyway? Isn't it yours? Then shouldn't you be the one to adjust your behavior, your style, in order to make your customer comfortable with you? Of course.

If I asked you which animal good salespeople are most like, what would you say? Some people think immediately of a lion, roaring through the jungle -- master of all he sees. Others say a fox, crafty and thoughtful. Still others say a dog, because of their loyalty and likeablity.

Illustration 6-1

None of these are my model. I like to think of good salespeople as being like chameleons. You're familiar with the chameleon. It's the lizard blessed with the unique ability to change colors to blend into its environment. If a chameleon is walking through green grass, it's green. If it's running across brown sand, it's brown.

Great salespeople have a similar ability. They reflect the behavioral style of their prospects and customers. Like the chameleon, they can "change colors" depending on the demands of the environment in which they find themselves. I call this skill "reflective behavior." It's the most sophisticated and powerful relationship-building skill.

As a professional salesperson intent on building relationships, it means that you take on the style with which the customer is most comfortable. If your customer is thoughtful and deliberate, somber and subdued, be the same things yourself. If your customer is quick and assertive, match his style quip for quip.

When I discuss this concept in my seminars, I often have someone respond with the question, "Isn't that phony?"

The answer is no. Think of yourself as a diamond. You can rotate the diamond to reflect certain facets of yourself that are already there. If you don't have it in you, you can't be something you're not. When you reflect a customer's unique style, you're choosing to reflect and emphasize a certain part of yourself. You're subjugating your own passing emotions for a decision of will to be disciplined in reflecting your customer's behavior style back to him or her.

We're not talking about issues of substance, we're talking about style. I'm not suggesting that if you're a Republican you pretend you're a Democrat. That's an issue of substance, and to do so would be dishonest. Focus on style, not substance.

Occasionally I'll be teaching this concept, and someone will say, " I have my own style of selling." My response? "Grow up." *Your* style isn't important. *Your customer's style is.* If you're going to be an effective salesperson in the Information Age, you're going to have to acquire an edge in a competitive, commoditicized world. That means making your customers comfortable with you, and that means reflecting your customer's style at the expense of your own. It's the mature, professional approach.

One more example. When I come home from work and see my wife on the phone, within a moment or two I can tell with whom she is talking. It has nothing to do with what she says, and everything to do with how she says it. She, like you, uses one mode of communication – tone of voice, expressions, etc – with our oldest son, another with our daughter, still another with our youngest son, and so on. She intuitively understands that the onus for effective communication rests with the communicator.

So, how do you do it?

You apply this principle in three ways: Reflecting your customer's communication style, language, and connections.

Communication Style

Everyone has a most comfortable style of communicating with other people. I recall a sales call I made to the regional vice-president of a national company. His office was in Fort Wayne, Indiana. I had a difficult time finding the office because I was expecting it to be in a modern office building. After all, he was responsible for all of his company's operations in one third of the country. Finally I located the address – an old, abandoned grocery store that had not been significantly renovated. It still had the imprint of the sign on the bricks and the old plate glass windows in the front. As I entered, I noticed that the old tile floor was still being used.

The receptionist directed me into the customer's office. As I entered, I noticed a modular office partition leaning up against the wall on my left. On it was tacked a sales chart. The walls were bare. No decorations, certificates, or photographs to be seen.

In the middle of the office was a metal desk, and in front of the desk, two chairs that did not match. The customer was wearing a suit and tie (the suit was buttoned). He looked up as I came in, extended his hand very formally, and said, "What can I do for you?"

Let's reflect on this situation. With what kind of communication style do you think this customer is most comfortable? Before we discuss that, let's look at another example.

This one was another sales call I made, on a person of a similar position – executive vice-president of a company of a similar size, in Grand Rapids, Michigan. As I was led into his office by the receptionist, I almost tripped on the carpeting, it was so thick. The corner of the office to my left was decorated with a number of photographs of his sons playing hockey. There were some home-made cards, the kind created in kindergarten classes, saying " I love you, Daddy," and decorated with crudely drawn hearts. Across the back wall was a wooden bookshelf, laden with knick-knacks and photographs. He had a rich, dark wooden desk, with two matching, thickly upholstered chairs. A sectional sofa hugged the wall across from his desk, and a coffee table with a coffee pot and cups sat on the table.

He had on a tie, but his coat was hanging on the back of his chair, and his sleeves were rolled up. As I entered the office, he came around the desk to greet me, shook my hand, put his other hand on my shoulder, guided me toward the sectional sofa, and said, "Sit down over here, and let's talk."

With what kind of communication style do you think he was most comfortable? Certainly not the same as the Ft. Wayne customer. And what kind of response would be most appropriate from me, if I'm going to be guided by the principle, "**People are most comfortable with people who are like themselves?"**

Everything about the environment and the personal appearance of the Ft. Wayne customer told me he was a "director." That's someone who is very formal, serious, business-like, task-oriented and to the point. My job, as a chameleon salesperson, is to reflect that style. When he greeted me with, "What can I do for you?" I responded with, "I have three items on the agenda. Here's the first."

I assessed his style, and reflected a communication style with which he was most comfortable.

On the other hand, everything about the other customer screamed "socializer" at me. That's someone who is friendly, very people-oriented, and is sensitive to the emotional side of interpersonal communications.

When he greeted me by directing me to the sofa, I began the conversation with, "It looks like your kids play hockey, right?" My job was to assess his most comfortable communication style, and reflect it.

Could you imagine me sitting down on the sofa and saying to him, "I have three items on the agenda, here's the first one?" Of course not. Regardless of my style, regardless of my agenda, that wouldn't have been his style.

You've got the idea. If you can accurately identify each of your customers' styles, you'll be able to reflect that style when you're with him/her. In so doing, you'll influence your customer to be comfortable with you.

This issue of communication style is a science that goes back several decades. A great deal of research has been done on it, a number of books have been written about it, and entire companies built around the concept.

Almost every author uses a different set of terms to express very similar concepts. For our purposes, let's assume that there are four basic types of communication styles. The two I've already mentioned, "director" and "socializer" as well as two others, "thinker," and "supporter." Here's a description of the most obvious characteristics of each.

>   Director – The primary communication need of this type is to dominate or control the interaction. They are formal, serious, and task-oriented. They'll tell you things, and get impatient with the details.
>
>   Socializer – Their primary communication need is to influence. They are very people oriented, open and sensitive to others. They like recognition, being with people, and are interested in the emotional component of communication.
>
>   Thinker – Their primary motivation is compliance. They are generally very slow to react, preferring to think things through. They are often formal and conservative in their attitudes and communication.
>
>   Supporters – Their primary motivation is steadiness. They are interested in numbers and facts, and are money and time oriented. They are the most risk-aversive of all the types.

As always, to implement the principle, you'll need to understand and use a "how-to" process. Here's a simple two-step process to help you implement this principle.

The Reflective Behavior Process
    1. Assess your customer
    2. Reflect your best understanding of his/her style.
   Here's how to implement these steps.

 Step One. Assess your customers.

    Human beings are fascinating creatures who can almost always be counted on to make their mark on their environment. That means that a person's work environment almost always reflects his/her personality. Your job, as a competent Six Hat Salesperson, is to quickly study your customer's environment so that you can pick up clues as to your customer's communication style.

    Reflect on the two examples I described above. The complete lack of decoration and the stark functionality of the environment of my Ft. Wayne customer told me, before I ever laid eyes on him, that he was a direct, to the point, task-oriented person.

    On the other hand, the warm, comfortable environment and overwhelming number of "people" decorations showed me that my other customer was a people person.

    As you initiate a sales call, discipline yourself to quickly study the environment of your customer to pick up those kinds of clues. Whenever possible, strive to have the meeting in the customer's personal work space. It won't do you much good, for example, to meet with a customer in a conference room that doesn't reflect your customer's personal presence, when you could have met in his/her office.

Study your customer's personal presentation. By that I mean the manner in which your customer has chosen to appear to you. Remember my Ft. Wayne customer's buttoned up look? And my Grand Rapids customer's sleeves rolled-up look? Both indications of their personal presentation.

Finally, assess their actual physical behavior. Body language can be enormously instructional. Mr. Ft. Wayne rose kind of stiffly and reached across the desk, keeping it between him and me. My Grand Rapids customer came around the desk, greeting me at the door, and put his hand on my shoulder – all indications of a "people-person" – a socializer.

Here are some clues to help you quickly assess your customer's communication style:

Directors – stark, functional environment; formal, conservative, "buttoned-up" personal presentation; stiff, aloof, "stand-offish" body language, direct eye-contact.

Socializers – warm, comfortable environments, with lots of evidence of people interests; often trendy clothing, warm personal presentation; close contact, open and sweeping gestures.

Thinkers – often cluttered environments; clothing often looks like an "afterthought" – doesn't always go together; asks a lot of questions, few hand gestures, not much eye contact.

Supporters – decorated environments – flowers, cards, etc.; soft, comfortable and often attractively dressed; non-aggressive body language.

Chapter Six: The Second Hat – Trusted Friend

 Step Two. Reflect your customer's style.
You've done a quick assessment of your customer's most comfortable style. Now, it's your job to reflect, or match that style. The easiest way to do this is to ask yourself how your customer would like to be dealt with. With what sort of style from you would he/she be most comfortable?

For example, if you peg your customer as a director, don't ask about his/her hobbies. That's much too personal. If you deem your customer to be a socializer, don't get right to the point. That's much too task-oriented.

I really can't give you a list of tactics, because people are too different. But I can urge you to be guided by the golden rule of behavior styles; communicate to your customer in the style in which your customer is most comfortable.

 Language
We've been discussing the process of reflecting behavioral styles as a way of making your customers comfortable with you. But behavioral styles aren't the only aspect of a customer's style with which you need to be concerned. Focus, also, on your customer's language. Use the customer's words, expressions, and cadences in talking with him/her, and you'll once again be perceived as being like your customer – someone with whom it is easy to be comfortable.

I recall a sales call made on a particularly good client. "Today in my business," he said to me, "it's like we're stuck in the middle of a fast moving river, trying to swim against the current of all these small orders we receive every day."

He could have described his business problem by talking about the numbers of orders he received, the overloaded customer service staff, and the backlog at the data-input desk. Instead, he chose to use an analogy.

My response? "It sounds like we should build some water sluices and dams to get control of the flow."

"That's it exactly!" he exclaimed.

I could have said that we needed to create policies and procedures to systematically screen and process those orders. But that would have been my terminology, not his. Instead, I chose to speak in his language, in the style to which he was most comfortable. That's an example of *reflecting your customer's language.*

Use the same two-step process, only apply it to language as well as communication style.

1. Assess your customer, and then
2. Reflect your customer's language.

This is a matter of listening, not just to what your customer is saying, but the actual words and expression with which it is being said.

Listen specifically to your customers' analogies. An analogy is a comparison. My customer in the example above chose to speak about his flow of orders by comparing it to the current in a river. Many of your customers will have favorite or comfortable analogies. When you explain your product or service in the terms of their analogies, they feel like you understand them and you're like them. You've made major steps forward in your attempt to make them comfortable with you.

Listen also to their expressions. People develop expressions and slang that arise out of their experience and their associations. When you use those same expressions you send the subconscious signal that you can relate to their experience and their environment.

Chapter Six: The Second Hat – Trusted Friend

Last year I presented a number of programs in Southern Africa. Early in the first program, one of the audience used the expression, "That's a real thumb-sucker." I was dumb-founded. What on earth did that mean? Everyone in the room seemed to accept his comment without hesitation, so I concluded that it must be a common expression. At the break, I asked a group what it meant, and then used it regularly throughout the balance of my seminars.

Finally, if you really want to become a sophisticated "reflective behavior" practitioner, listen to your customer's cadences. A cadence is the rhythm to a person's speech. Some people speak slowly, other's rapidly. Some accentuate certain parts of a sentence, others don't. Each person has a unique rhythm. Concentrate on picking up on that cadence, and using a similar rhythm in your conversation. Remember the two step process – assess, and reflect.

Connections

You've heard the expression, "Birds of a feather flock together." Applied to people, not birds, it means that people who are alike tend to go to the same place, be interested in the same things, join the same organizations, etc.

You're thinking, "So what?" Here's what. The obverse is also true. "If birds flock together, they are probably of the same feather." Applied to people, it means that if people have the same things in common – if they go to the same places, if they are interested in the same things, if they join the same organizations, then they are probably a lot alike.

So, if you want your customer to become comfortable with you by seeing you as like him/her, then make sure you point out those things (connections) that you have in common with your customer. The more people, places, organizations, and experiences you have in common with your customer, the more he/she perceives you to be like them.

As you may have guessed by now, you use the same two-step process to implement this concept.
1. Assess your customer.
2. Reflect your customer's connections by mentioning them.

Study your customer's work environment, personal presentation, language, stories, illustrations, etc., and find some things that you have in common. You may have been to the same place, traveled or gone on vacations to the same area, gone to the same church, rooted for the same sports teams, belonged to the same civic organizations, have seen the same movies, read the same books, seen the same plays, or known the same people. Got the idea? The sooner you find something you have in common, the sooner you'll be able to put the prospect at ease and make him/her comfortable with you. After you've found something you have in common, work them into the conversation as early as you can.

Here's a real life example from my own experience.

I went into a man's office, a CEO of a small business, to meet him for the first time. I was there to discuss sales training. He asked if I wanted a cup of coffee. By the way, I always take a cup of coffee, even if I've just come from a breakfast meeting, and I've had six cups of coffee already and I am beginning to sweat and wonder where the restroom is.

There's a reason for that. Think about what happens when you say, "Yes, I'll have a cup of coffee." Your host has to arrange for it. He has to either get the coffee, or instruct

Chapter Six: The Second Hat – Trusted Friend

someone else to get it. In either case, he has to take a few moments to attend to the task. While he's doing that, you can use that time to look around the office and find something in which to be interested.

That's exactly what happened. When he was out making arrangements for coffee, I spotted a large photograph of a sailboat. I sail. So, I immediately chose that as the item in which I would be interested, and my point of common ground.

When he came in and handed me the coffee, the first thing I did was point at the photograph and say, "You sail?" He replied, "Yes, that's my boat." The photograph was large enough that I could make out the name of the boat. It was "Kelly Ann." I have a daughter named Kelly Ann. Which is what I said to him next. And he said, "I have daughter named Kelly Ann." This boat was named after her.

At that point, the conversation turned to daughters and sailing, and we achieved a real, common bond based on our similar interests and experiences. None of this would have happened had I not disciplined myself to find common ground.

Which brings us to a very special kind of "connection" you can make with your customers. That's the connection of one, real, live, human being to another. Here's the issue -- when you meet a customer for the first time, particularly in the first few minutes of your visit, he/she tends to treat you as a stereotype. You're a "salesperson," not a real person. As long as you allow yourself to be treated as a stereotype, you'll maintain a superficial, stereotypical relationship. You need to make a "real human-being" connection with him. You need to break through the stereotype and cause your customers to see you as a person. You make this connection, breaking though the wall between your customer and yourself, by sharing something unique and personal about yourself.

Here's an example. During the first few minutes of most meetings I have with a new prospect, I try to work into the conversation the fact that my wife and I are foster parents. We have, over the years, cared for 18 foster children.

You're probably asking what that has to do with sales. My answer is, "Nothing." But if you ask what it has to do with creating a relationship with the prospect, getting him to see me as a real, live human being, then I'd say it has *everything* to do with that.

You see, once I share something unique and personal about myself, that I'm a foster father, the prospect can no longer treat me as a stereotype. He now sees me as a *real* person with *real* blood flowing through my veins. I've connected to the "humanness" in him/her. You can do the same thing.

Let's summarize. Influencing your customer to be comfortable with you, an essential Six Hat Salesperson competency, is a matter of helping him see you as being like him. Your primary process is that of assessing and then reflecting your customers' communication style, language and connections.

Now, we're ready to work on the other two aspects of the second hat: influencing your customer to trust and respect you.

Chapter Seven:
Gaining Your Customer's Trust and Respect

Remember the primary principle anchoring this hat? *People buy from people with whom they are comfortable, who they trust and respect.* Not only must you make your customers comfortable with you, you must also influence them to respect you (to see you as competent) as well as to trust you. When your customers see you as a competent person they can trust, the buying decision becomes less of a risk.

Let's consider the principles and processes for each of these issues, beginning with influencing your customers to perceive you as competent.

People perceive you as competent, not so much by what you say, but rather by what you ask. Did you ever go to a new physician for the first time, and have him/her ask you for an incredibly detailed health history? He puts you through the wringer inquiring about all the little details of every illness or health incident you've had. By the time you are finished, you are exhausted. And you leave the office thinking to yourself, "Boy, was he good."

What made you think that? Was it what he said, or what he asked? Obviously, it was his detailed and knowledgeable questions.

Here's another example. Suppose you're having difficulty with your automobile, so you take it into the mechanic down the street. You notice a neon sign in his window announcing "Computer diagnostics." On the walls of his reception room hang several certificates.

You say, "I'm having trouble with my automobile. It's making a funny noise."

"We're all certified," he says, "and we have computer diagnostics. Leave it here and pick it up at 5 PM."

You aren't totally sold, so you go across the street to the competing mechanic there. You notice there is no sign in the window, nor certificates on the wall.

You say the same thing to the mechanic. "I'm having trouble with my automobile. It's making a funny noise."

"What kind of noise?" he asks.

"It's a strange thumping sound" you reply.

"Can you describe it?"

"It sounds like something metal banging against something else."

"Where is it coming from?"

"Someplace in the front, sounds like more to the passenger side of the car."

"What kind of car do you have?" he asks.

"90 Taurus."

"90 Taurus, huh. OK, tell me, when you drive faster, does the thumping increase it's rate also?"

"Well, now that you mention it, I believe it does."

"OK," he says. "And do you hear the sound when the car is cold, just after you start it in the morning, as well as when it's hot?"

"Actually," you say, "I don't think it does happen when it's cold."

"OK," he says, "Leave it here and pick it up at 5 PM."

With which one of the two mechanics do you leave your car? Silly question. Everyone I know says they'd leave it with the second mechanic. Why? Because he obviously knows what he's doing.

And what made you think that he knows what he's doing?

It's his questions! We understand that it takes greater competence to ask good questions about a situation than it does to make pithy statements.

If you want your customers to respect your competence, ask good questions.

Here's a process to help you put this principle into practice. Let's call it the *perception of competence* process.

1. Consider each of your products and/or services.
2. Focusing on each one, identify the details of your customer's situations which would make them want your offerings.
3. Brainstorm a set of questions that would reveal those details.
4. Rewrite and edit those questions to reveal your understanding of the customer's experiences, objectives, problems, and feelings.
5. Use those questions.

Let's think through an example.

Step One. Consider each of your products and/or services.

My company sells a number of products and services. For purposes of this example, let's focus on one which every reader of this book will appreciate: customized sales training.

Step Two. Focusing on each one, identify the details of your customer's situations which would make them want your offerings.

A company interested in customized sales training would...
- have a sufficient quantity of outside salespeople, probably a minimum of 15 or so.
- be interested in improving the productivity and/or performance of those people.
- believe that their salespeople could learn something from a training program.
- probably have invested in packaged programs or public seminars in the past, and now are looking for a more individualized approach.
- be willing and ready to pay for it.

Step Three. Brainstorm a set of questions that would reveal those details.

We'll go into more detail on creating questions when we consider the third hat. We could create dozens if not hundreds of possibilities for each of the issues above, but for the purposes of this illustration, we'll focus on just one of those issues, "be interested in improving the performance of the salespeople." Let's assume that you've generated a set of questions that includes the following:

What makes you interested in customized sales training?
How is your company doing relative to the competition?
How is your company doing relative to its goals and objectives?
What would improved sales performance mean to your company?
What makes you think that your salespeople could improve?

Having generated or brainstormed a series of questions, you're now ready to move to the next step in the process.

Step Four. Rewrite and edit those questions to reveal your understanding of the customer's experiences, objectives, problems, and feelings.

These questions are designed to convey to your customer the perception that you understand his/her situation. That situation consists of your customer's experiences, objectives, problems, and feelings. Let's take one of our first set of questions, and work with it to convey these kinds of perceptions.

Let's begin with, "What would improved sales performance mean to your company?"

Suppose we turned that into...

"I imagine that you have some sales goals that are a bit of a stretch for you, right?"

"What sort of experience have you had with sales training in the past?"

"Most companies who are talking to us about improved sales performance have come to the conclusion that either they don't have the resources to do it themselves, or that it would be too costly in terms of time and money to attempt it. Would either of those circumstances describe your situation?"

"I'll bet you're frustrated with some of the things you see your sales people doing, aren't you?"

Now, you may want to take exception to some of the language in these questions. However, the overall perception they'll convey to your customers is that you understand their situation. In other words, you know what you're doing. In other words, you must be a competent salesperson. In other words, it's less risk dealing with you than it is with someone of less competence.

Step Five. Use those questions.

It doesn't do any good to prepare them if you never discipline yourself to use them. Again, we'll discuss more details of using questions in chapter ten. For now, let me just encourage you to begin using the questions you've created by using this process.

As a result, your customers will see you as competent. They'll be more inclined to deal with you, and you'll gain a competitive edge, and greater competency at the Second Hat – becoming a trusted friend.

There's yet one more component of this Hat – influencing your customers to trust you.

Gaining Your Customer's Trust

In my first professional sales position, I discovered that honesty and integrity were not just moral imperatives, they were highly prized qualities that prospects and customers valued. That meant ethics and integrity were also good business.

Everyone would rather work with honest, trustworthy people than with people who are dishonest and untrustworthy. Wouldn't you? If you're going to be someone with whom your customers want to work, you need to rigorously adhere to a consistent set of ethics. Which brings us to the next principle: **People trust people who have integrity.**

A good starting point is focusing on integrity. Webster's defines integrity as: "intactness, firmness of character." It is this *firmness of character* that is the overarching quality that transcends everything you do, if

Chapter Seven: Gaining Your Customer's Trust & Respect

you want to earn your customer's trust. It gives shape and substance to the more specific list of ethical commandments that follows. Firmness of character, translated into your sales behavior, means that you do what you say you're going to do, and that you are what you portray yourself to be. In other words, your customers and your colleagues can count on you to act honestly and consistently. They trust you. The salespeople who earn their customers' trust by being people of character, and people of integrity, have an immeasurable edge over the competition.

Not long ago, I was financing a new marketing project by selling limited partnership investments. I decided to offer these investments to the people who knew me the best, and who were acquainted with my work: my clients. So I organized a number of small investor information meetings with groups of my clients. At one of the meetings, during the informal question and answer session that followed my presentation, one of my clients announced that, regardless of the details of the investment, he knew me to be a man of integrity, and that was good enough for him. Another chimed right in and agreed, saying he had confidence in my integrity also.

I was touched. I told them both that their comment was one of the highest complements they could pay me. Their trust in my integrity sure made doing business together much easier.

Integrity -- being a person of solid, reliable character - is the overarching concept for all the specific ethical guidelines that follow. It's a quality of character that emanates out of you like light reflected from a diamond. In fact, a diamond is a great visual image to convey the concept of integrity.

Chapter Seven: Gaining Your Customer's Trust & Respect

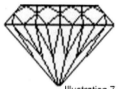
Illustration 7-1

A diamond is one of the hardest substances known to man. It's almost impossible to make a dent in one. For hundreds and thousands of years, a diamond can remain the same. That's like integrity, which doesn't change, but remains solid and not subject to the temptations that swirl around it.

A diamond purely reflects any light that shines on it. A salesperson with integrity makes everyone look good – the customers, bosses, support staff and associates.

A diamond is of great value. And so is integrity. As a sales consultant, I'm often asked what one should look for when contemplating hiring a salesperson. My reply is always the same. More than skill or knowledge, you should look for qualities of character. And there is no quality of character more valuable to a salesperson than integrity. It's the first quality to look for when you're hiring salespeople.

One of the services I provide my clients is to interview a prospective salesperson, offering my client a second opinion as to the suitability of that individual. In one case I interviewed a candidate for a position as a mortgage originator. In the course of the conversation, the candidate confided in me that, since he had recently moved to West Michigan from a much larger metropolitan area, he discovered that pay scales were less here than where he came from. So, he changed his salary history on his resume and application form, stating that he had made less than he really did. His reasoning was that if a potential employer in West Michigan saw how much he had made, they would never be able to pay him that much, and he wouldn't get the job.

That all sounded reasonable. I could certainly understand his reasoning. The only problem was that his actions revealed a lack of integrity. He lied on the resume, he lied on the application, and he lied to my client in the interview process. Regardless of how well meaning and reasonable the lie was, it was still a lie. I immediately decided to recommend that he not be hired. If a person would lie on the resume, he'd lie to his boss and he'd lie to his customers.

I'm going to vary from my general approach in that I'm not going to discuss processes for implementing this principle. There isn't any process for ethical behavior. Rather, there is a set of rules. To be seen as a trustworthy person, follow these nine commandments.

The Nine Commandments for the Ethical Salesperson

1. Don't intentionally misrepresent anything.

Never, never, never lie to a customer. About anything. Period.

2. Fix any important misunderstandings that you can.

It's possible that your customer will form incorrect ideas about some of the products you represent or the services that come with them. It's also possible that they will misunderstand things about your competitors, and about the needs and statements of other people who work in their organizations.

It's very tempting, when these misunderstandings work in your favor, to ignore them. However, that's not dealing with integrity. When you become aware of any significant misunderstandings your customer has that impacts the buying decision or the larger relationship, you need to correct them. Now, this doesn't mean that you need to set him straight on his political beliefs or his views on the controversial call in Sunday's football game. But it does mean that, on the important issues that affect the sale, allowing misunderstandings to exist is an act, on your part, of passive dishonesty. Correct them when you can.

3. Work hard for your employer.

It's easy for a salesperson to give in to the temptation to cut corners when it comes to working a full day, every day. After all, who really knows if you hit your first call at 9:00 A.M. instead of 8:30 A.M.? And who knows if you take a 30-minute coffee break between calls? And who knows if you make it home by 3:00 P.M. some days, and take a number of afternoons off to visit the golf course or the fishing hole during the summer?

All of these examples are ways of shortchanging your employer that, in all probability, no one will ever know about except you.

And that's my point. *You* will know. A code of ethics is easy to live by when everyone is watching. But it's a real test of character when your ethics are tested in situations where noone else knows, and you know you can get away with it.

You owe your employer consistent, full days of your best efforts. Anything less is unethical.

4. If ethics are at stake, always be willing to trade a short term loss for the sake of a long-term gain.

This may be another definition of integrity -- the courage and conviction to walk away from an unethical short-term gain in return for a long-term gain. In other words, always be willing to give up a sale or some immediate advantage if you must stretch the truth or act unethically to get it.

For example, you may have an opportunity to acquire a quick sale because your customer has misunderstood the specifications or features of your product. It's tempting to take the order and not say anything. But that would not be ethical.

The ethical salesperson will correct the customer and lose the immediate gain that the sale would have brought. The payoff, however, is the long-term gain in your reputation for integrity.

A long-term gain achieved ethically is always worth more than *any* short-term advantage.

5. Do what you say you are going to do.

This isn't as simple as it sounds. One of the obvious implications of doing what you say you're going to do is that you must not say you are going to do something that you know you can't do. In other words, don't over promise. That's difficult to do when you're in the middle of a competitive situation over a nice piece of business, and you know the competition is over promising to get the sale. But, if you're going to be an ethical salesperson, you won't over promise, because you know you won't be able to do what you say you're going to do.

There's another implication -- you must be organized enough to follow through on your promises. The most honest person in the world can be perceived as unreliable if he is not organized enough to follow through on his promises. If you say you're going to call a customer back on Thursday, make sure that you have a tickler file, day-time planner, computer program, or some other system that will remind you to call them back when Thursday comes. That's being ethical.

6. Give liberally.

As a professional salesperson, you enjoy a challenging job with a lot of freedom and a substantial income level. The world is full of people who would love to have that. You're one of life's more fortunate people.

I think that means that you have a greater than average responsibility to give back to society. Give of your money freely to charitable or religious causes, and give liberally of your time and expertise to the organizations that you can help. Your expertise, your time, your people skills, your organizational skills, and your confidence and ability to get things done – all of these are assets you can bring to the Boy Scouts, your church, the PTA, and a thousand other organizations that can use your abilities.

Since you are more blessed with talent, time, and money than most of the population, you have a greater responsibility to use it for purposes other than just your own edification. Nido Quebin said "Service to others is the rent you pay for taking up space on this earth. The richer the space, the higher the rent." Give liberally.

7. Recognize those who help you.

It's easy to get into the mind-set that you alone are responsible for your success. After all, you're out there all alone, fighting the battle every day. Nobody else knows what good work you did in getting that account, or how hard it is some days when nothing goes your way.

In spite of this, you couldn't do your job without the support of a whole group of people back at the office. Your manager gave you an opportunity and nurtured you along. The inside people have cleaned up more than a few of your messes, and they have positively impacted many of your customers. Others have put lots of time and energy into creating the products that ultimately provide your livelihood.

All of these people, and probably dozens of others, have contributed in significant ways to your success. It is just as dishonest to not recognize them as it is to misrepresent a product.

The ethical salesperson recognizes those people who have helped him.

8. Never give up.

This may seem odd in a section on ethics, but I believe that giving up is the same thing as going home early or taking extra days off without anybody's approval. Both shortchange yourself as well as your employer.

When you give up prematurely on a sale, or you give up on yourself and give into negative thinking, you're choosing to deprive yourself and your employer of the full benefit of your talent and time. That's unethical.

9. Don't speak badly about anyone.

In my first sales position, when I was selling amplification equipment, there were 29 major installations purchased in my territory. I got the order in 28 of those deals. My stomach still gets a little tight whenever I remember one of my crucial sales calls with the 29th customer.

During the course of the conversation, she stopped me and said, "You know, I really don't like it that you're so negative about your competitor." I was stunned, embarrassed, and flustered. I turned beet red, and stumbled out an apology. But that was the end of that deal.

All because I had spoken badly about my competitor. That was an intensely painful lesson for me. I resolved never to make that mistake again.

As I matured, I realized that, when you negatively judge anyone, you really say more about yourself than you do about the other person. Speaking badly about a competitor, your boss, your company, or another customer, always makes you look bad. And besides, it's unethical.

Trying on the Second Hat

So, I have you convinced and a little overwhelmed. How do you take these principles, and processes and make them a part of your every day routine? Here are the principles we considered:

1. People find reasons to buy from people they trust, and with whom they are comfortable and confident.
2. Relationships save the customer time and mitigate the risk.
3. People are comfortable with people who are like themselves.
4. People perceive you as competent, not so much by what you say, but rather by what you ask.
5. People trust people who have integrity.

We articulated the processes that will help you unleash the power of those principles. Those include:
- the reflective process

o the perception of competency process

And then, of course, there were the nine commandments for ethical behavior.

Where to start? Here. Make a hard and fast, absolute decision – a decision that you will never reconsider. The decision? You will deal with integrity in every situation. Period. No questions, no limitations, no exceptions. Once you've made that decision, you won't have to wrestle with every decision and every temptation. You will have already made the decision once and for all. Believe me, it's a whole lot easier and less stressful in the long run to make that decision and then to never quibble over it again, then it is to give yourself lots of room for maneuvering. When you do that, you struggle over every decision.

So, begin with integrity. You'll find that decision impacting your routine and your relationships almost daily.

Now that you know where you stand, you begin to focus on your customer in a more sensitive fashion. Take one of the three areas for reflective behavior – behavior style, language, or connections – and begin to play with it. Decide to focus on that one area for a month or two, and see how much sharper you can become at both assessing and reflecting. When you feel that you're doing it naturally, without having to think about it, move on to another area.

The competency questions will require more structured work. You may want to talk with your manager about it. This really is a great project for a group of you and your colleagues to work on together. Suggest to your manager that under his/her guidance, the group could develop a set of competency questions that everyone could use. Then, plug away at it, one product or service at a time.

If that approach doesn't appeal to you, then pick one product to focus on and spend a couple of weeks working on the competency questions for that product. As you experiment with them, you'll find it easier and easier to create similar questions for the other products or services you represent.

And that will get you off to a great start in making this hat fit.

Wearing the Hat

When you've fully incorporated these competencies, you'll find your confidence skyrocketing, and your sales paralleling that trajectory. Here's what you'll be doing...

You'll be confidently able to meet and interact with any person, no matter what their personality or background, because you'll be reflecting their styles, language and connections in a professional, disciplined fashion. Not only that, but you'll be getting most of the deals where there appears to be little difference between your offering and your competitor's. Your relationships will be the tie breaker.

You'll feel better about yourself, because you'll recognize that you are becoming perceived as a person of integrity. You'll enjoy the growing reputation as someone who is competent and trustworthy. Your customers will refer you to others, and look for reasons to do business with you.

You will have become a Trusted Friend. You will have taken your performance Up-a-Notch!

Chapter Eight:
Using the Six Hats to Take Your Performance Up-A-Notch

Challenge: Voice Mail is driving me crazy! It seems like I can never get through to the people I want to talk to.

Welcome to the club. Not so many years ago, there was no such thing as voice mail. Today, it is almost impossible to call a customer on the phone and get directly to him.

The electronic gatekeeper, voice mail, stands in the way. Voice mail has become the number one irritant for salespeople in the Information Age

And with good reason. If you can't communicate with your customers, you can't get to see them. And if you can't get to see them, you've been knocked out of the sales process. Unless you learn to work electronically, the likelihood of you making a sale is dramatically reduced.

So, voice mail is one of those irritating issues that threaten the very heart of what you do. You've got to solve the voice mail dilemma or you won't be in business very long.

Applying the Hats.

Let's begin by putting on the first hat, Astute Planner. Recognize that voice mail is one of the most likely outcomes of your telephone call. So, don't be surprised when you call a customer and are routed to voice mail. Instead, be prepared. Imagine that you are given the ability to create a 30 second radio commercial and beam it directly to your customer. What would be in that commercial?

That's the attitude to take. So, before you make each telephone call, prepare a 30 second radio commercial (your voice mail message). Then you're prepared for the likely occurrence of being routed to a voice mail system.

Next, put on the third hat, Skillful Influencer. You must put as much skill into your voice mail message as possible, influencing the customer to take action. It's important to focus on the action that you want the customer to take. If you're cold calling for a first appointment, the action you want the customer to take is to get back to you, either in person or via email or fax. If you're following up on a proposal or a previous visit, you want a different action from the customer. Keep clearly in mind the action you want them to take, and bring all your skills of influencing, using the presentation process as best you can, to deliver a powerful presentation. Don't sell your product, sell a return call. Give them a reason to call you back.

The presentation, like all of them, should traverse through the steps of the presentation process. Identify some need/interest you believe your customer has, identify some thing you can do to assist him, show him how that will benefit him, and ask for action. Use your language and tone of voice to convey competence and confidence and to make your customer comfortable with you. It's the influencing-presentation process capsulized in 30 seconds.

As long as you have your Skillful Influencer hat on, you can use it to take a broader view of the situation and create a series of communications of which your voice mail message is merely one piece.

As you know, the object of your efforts is to influence the customer to take action. In this case, the action is to call you back and/or to make an appointment to see you.

Think about using alternate media to make a series of contacts with the customer, to precondition him/her to respond to your call. For example, you may send a letter, follow it with an email, follow that with a fax, and then make your phone call.

A few years ago, one of my clients, an advertising agency, developed an incredibly creative way to precondition the customer to accept the initial phone call. Here's how the program worked. They first qualified a list of 100 people they wanted to see. During the first week of the program, they sent each of the 100 a small box, wrapped in plain brown paper, with a hand-printed address on it, and no return address. In the box was a sugar cube with a small printed message saying, "Keep it sweet." Nothing else. You can imagine the curious response of the people receiving that box.

The second week, another package came in the mail. It was wrapped and addressed in the same way, only this time, the box contained a lemon. The message read, "Don't let it go sour."

Week three came, and a third box arrived. Same wrapping, same appearance. This package contained some tinsel foil with the message, "Make it sparkle." Week four arrived, and the anticipated delivery of the fourth box. In it was the business card of the salesperson with a note, "I'll be calling you for an appointment." You may be interested in the result. One hundred percent of the recipients of that series of packages set appointments with the sales reps. The negative effect of voice mail was overcome by creatively pre-conditioning the customer to respond to your call.

But there are frequent occasions when you encounter voice mail and you're well down the rode of the sales process. It's not your first call, it's a subsequent visit with a customer you know. If you find yourself in this situation, apply all the strategies and tactics of the skillful infuencer.

However, you're best strategy is to apply the hat of Human Resource manager, focusing on time management issues. Think ahead and avoid voice mail altogether. When you're with the customer, instead of agreeing to call him and make an appointment for the next meeting, make the appointment now. Explain that doing so, even if it is tentative and several months in the future, will save you both a phone call or two, and that means less time and less hassle for both of you. When you make the appointment, you've eliminated the need for a phone call and the frustration of voice mail.

Even if the situation or one of your schedules change, you can then use voice mail to your advantage by calling with a schedule change, leaving that message, and getting your customer's acknowledgment on *your* voice mail!

Chapter Nine:
The Third Hat - Effective Consultant

What does it mean to be a consultant? Some people say a consultant is someone who borrows your watch, tells you what time it is and then charges you for it. As a consultant myself, I'd prefer a more positive definition. A consultant is someone you pay to understand you and your situation, and then to help you overcome problems and achieve objectives.

Notice, first, that there is a price. You must think highly enough of the consultant's capabilities to pay for them. People who work for free are generally worth exactly what you paid them.

One major thing you expect of consultants, whether personal therapists, business consultants, financial consultants, management consultants, even sales consultants, is that they take the time to understand you and your situation. How else can they provide you any direction or any assistance unless they understand who you are and with what issues you're struggling?

Then, you expect them to help you with your problems and your objectives. Notice that there is both a positive and negative here. Sometimes you'll employ a consultant to help you with your problems, but other times your investment is even more valuable when the consultant helps you achieve your objectives.

So what does all this have to do with selling in general, and the Six Hat Salesperson specifically? Only this: In the Information Age, more and more of your customers want you to be a consultant to them. Put yourself in their shoes. Growing complexity, increasing competition, time constraints – all these conspire to pressure them. Many of your customers have too much to do and not enough time in which to do it. So, they instinctively look for someone who can take some of the burden off of them – someone who understands their situation, and helps them sort through it all to assist them to solve their problems and achieve their objectives. They may not admit it, or even be aware of it, but that instinct to delegate or download is a real part of every decision.

You can be that consultant to many of your customers. You can understand them better than anyone else, and then use that deeper and more detailed understanding to help them solve their problems and achieve their objectives. You're paid, not in hourly billable time, but in sales commissions.

But becoming a consultant to your customers is not just an effective competency because of your customers' situations. If you only look at the competency from the salesperson's perspective, it is still an incredibly effective competency. That's because the largest, most important part of the sales process is accomplished when you understand the customer.

There was a time, in the product-focused days gone by, when understanding the customer was less important than understanding your product. Those days were

Chapter Nine: The Third Hat – Effective Consultant

squeezed into oblivion by the vice created by the proliferation of 'me too' products.

In a world where products and services are more and more alike, the power has moved from the product to the customer. In the Information Age, 75% of the successful sale lies in understanding the customer.

Apply the principles and practices of the second hat, Effective Consultant, and your sales performance will take a quantum leap forward.

No matter what you're selling, you can take on the role of the consultant to achieve Information Age success for you and your company.

Here's an example of how this idea of being a consultant to your customer can be applied even in a very simple selling situation.

Suppose you work in a retail store, selling women's dresses. A customer walks in, and begins examining a rack of evening dresses. You could approach her and say something like, "We've got some new designer dresses on this rack in back." That would be an example of a traditional, product-centered approach. You're focused on the products, the designer dresses, and don't take the time to understand the person.

On the other hand, you could take the "consultant" approach. You could say something like this, "Are you just looking for a nice dress, or do you have some specific occasion in mind?"

Your customer replies, "I've got a fancy company banquet to attend."

"Oh," you reply with a smile, " and what kind of impression do you want to make?"

Your customer smiles at you, "Something a little more eye-catching and a bit richer than everyone else."

"I imagine you'd look good in red," you say. "What other colors do you wear well?"

"Deep colors," she says. "You know, dark green, navy, black."

"I think I might have just the thing for you. Come back here and let me show you these new designer dresses."

Which of the two approaches do you think will provide the best results? Silly question. When you take the extra moment or two, and spend the extra bit of energy to understand your customers first, and then assist them with their problems and objectives, you'll find them to be much more receptive.

If you can apply the "consultant" hat in this simple, brief selling encounter, think of the potential in longer more complex selling situations.

Got the idea? The third hat, Effective Consultant, can be one of your most powerful competencies. Let's examine the first principle. **Your customers want to be understood.**

There is something in human beings that hungers to be understood. This is especially true when we're considering a high risk decision. Sometimes this hunger is almost visceral, deep down beneath our consciousness. At other times, we're very aware of our desire to be understood. Regardless, it's always there.

I'm reminded of Steven Covey's great challenge, from *The Seven Habits of Highly Effective People*, "Seek first to understand, and then to be understood." What a great expression of this Hat, and this first principle.

In the past few months, my wife and I have been considering remodeling our house. We've called four companies, all referrals or recommendations to us. Salespeople from two of the four actually showed up. The salesperson from the first company looked at our sketches, listened to us for a few minutes, and then got a window sample from his car and spent the next 30 minutes presenting that window to us. We didn't buy. We were looking for a deck with French doors opening onto it, not new windows. This salesperson was obviously product-focused, a window salesperson, not a "consultant."

The second salesperson spent almost an hour with us, asking about what we had in mind, suggesting ideas and getting our response, and getting to know what we are really looking for.

He's due back in a week or so with a proposal. I don't think he'll bring a window sample with him. I do think that he'll have a proposal that we'll seriously consider, and we are, at this point, inclined to do business with him. Why? Because he took the time and invested the energy to understand us and our situation.

From our perspective as buyers, we're favorably impressed with salespeople who take the time to understand us. The same thing is true of your customers. As complexity and confusion grow in their business lives, they're more and more favorably impressed with salespeople who take the time to understand them.

It's a bit more complicated than that, however, from the point of view of the salesperson. Which brings us to the second principle: **Understanding your customer is like peeling an onion.**

I know, that's one of the craziest things you've heard. Trust me for a minute, as we consider this principle.

Suppose you've just come back from your company's annual sales meeting. For three days, you sat in meetings and ate hotel food. Now, you're home, and you'd like nothing more than a cold beer and a home-cooked meal.

You suggest a big salad for dinner, and your spouse agrees, suggesting that you peel the onion.

So, you get out a big, fat Bermuda onion, one of those that are about the size of a softball. You position it carefully on a cutting board, and root through the drawer until you find a sharp meat cleaver. Steadying the onion with one hand, you raise the meat cleaver above your head, and, with a karate-type movement, smash the meat cleaver neatly into the center of the onion, splitting it evenly in two.

You pick up one of the onion halves and examine it from the inside. You note that it has layers and layers, each deeper and more tightly compressed than the one surrounding it. You begin to peel the onion, stripping off the skin. As you pull off the skin of the onion, you notice that the skin is thin, dry, and crinkely, with very little scent. However, as you peel each layer, one at a time, you soon come to the conclusion that each layer is more strongly scented than the one above it, and that the strength of the onion's pungency comes from the inside out. Got the image?

Good. That's the best way to understand this principle. Just like there are layers and layers to an onion, so there are layers and layers to your customer. Just like the superficial layers of an onion are thin and mild, so too, the superficial levels of your customers have little strength. But as you peel the onion deeper and deeper, the strength increases. So, too, with your customer.

Let's apply this specifically to understanding your customer in a sales situation. Look at illustration number 9-1. Imagine it to be a slice of that onion. On the very surface are the technical specifications for the product or service the customer wants. For example, let's say you call on one of your customers and he says, "I need to purchase three green

Chapter Nine: The Third Hat - Effective Consultant

metal widgets that are 1/2" by 6". Many salespeople would say, "OK, they are $2.50 each." In this example, the salesperson understood the customer at the most superficial level -- technical specifications-- and responded in kind.

PEELING THE ONION

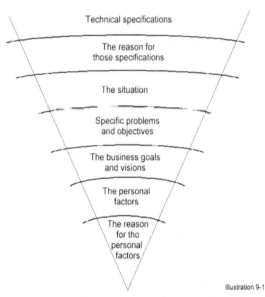

Illustration 9-1

But you can go deeper in understanding the customer by discovering the reason behind those specifications.

Our rep, when confronted with the same request, may say, "What are you going to use them for?" or "Is there a reason you asked for metal instead of plastic?" This kind of response will uncover the next level, the *reason* for the specifications.

There's more. *Situation* refers to the history behind the need, and the circumstances surrounding the need. For example, let's say that our salesperson now replies, "John, what's your situation? Why is this an issue now?" When the customer replies to that question, he has uncovered a deeper layer of need.

Yet you're still pretty close to the surface. When you uncover the specific problems and objectives which underlay the original request, you've gotten deeper in your understanding of the customer. Back to our example. Suppose your customer says, "We're having a problem with our second shift production. The line keeps breaking down. Our maintenance supervisor wants to stockpile some of the parts that he has been regularly replacing."

Now you have an understanding of the specific problems and objectives. There is more. Suppose you ask how that problem affects the rest of the company. And suppose your customer explains the effect of the breakdown on production, net profits, and overtime pay for the second shift. Now you understand the customer at yet a deeper level.

But you can go deeper still. When you ask how those systematic problems affect his business goals, and you learn that it's particularly troublesome because your customer's goals are to increase net profits by five percent this year, you understand the customer at an even deeper level.

You take a significant plunge deeper when you are able to understand how the situation affects the individual with whom you're talking. For example, when you know him well enough to ask, "John, how can I make you look good in this transaction?" and get an honest response, you've penetrated to a new layer of understanding.

Finally, when you understand the individual motivations -- the reasons for the personal factors -- you understand the customer at levels that few salespeople ever approach. That's where the masters work. Those motivations are often emotionally driven. So, when you understand the customer's emotions – how the situation makes him/her feel, you've arrived at the heart of the onion. The Six Hat salesperson understands this similarity between peeling an onion and understanding your customer. Bring these two principles together and the results can be amazingly powerful.

Let me give you two easy-to-remember acronyms to help you work with these principles: SPOO, and PIE. SPOO stands for the customer's *specific problems or objectives*. In order to peel the onion and understand your customer, you must get to this level by uncovering these two issues.

Most salespeople consider themselves to be problem-solvers. They find an opportunity to sell their products or services when their customers have problems to solve. That's fine, as far as it goes. But just as important as helping your customers solve their problems is helping your customers achieve their objectives. Focusing on understanding your customer's objectives opens up at least as many opportunities for you to sell your products and services, and forces you to understand what is important to your customers.

For example, you may be selling production equipment. If your customer doesn't have any problems with the current state of the production line, you may think you have no opportunities to sell your products. But, if you were to peel the onion and discuss with your customer his/her objectives, you may find that the company wants to have a 15% increase in capacity over the next 12 months. That's an objective, not a problem, and it's a great opportunity for you. Until you understand both sides of the picture, the customer's specific problems or objectives, you can't really function as a consultant to your customers. Remember, SPOO.

Then, remember PIE. Not apple pie, but rather a simplified illustration of the onion. Here's an easy-to-remember and easy-to-use version. Note that illustration 9-2 simplifies the original onion to three levels. The most superficial is *problems or objectives.* I know, to be consistent I should label this SIE. But, I'm taking editorial license in order to create an easy-to-remember acronym. P works better than S.

THE CUSTOMER'S PIE

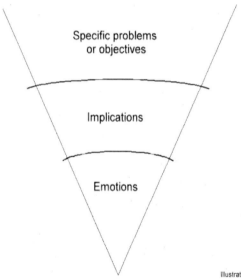

Illustration 9-2

The second layer down consists of the *implications.* In other words, you take the time to understand the consequences of successfully solving the problem or meeting the objective, as well as the consequences of not doing so. You probe those consequences or implications on the company as well as the individuals with whom you are working.

For example, you may have discovered a customer wants to increase the production capacity by 15%. When you enter into a discussion with that company that causes you to understand the consequences to the company of not increasing capacity, and the ramifications of doing so, that's good. When you understand what those consequences are for the individuals within the company, you've just peeled the onion a little deeper.

For example, your customer may say, "If we don't get the 15% increase in capacity, we'll not be able to handle the new contract from Ford. And if we can't handle the new contract, they could very well take our current business away from us, because they want to consolidate vendors. That's a major portion of our business. If that goes, we'd have a difficult time surviving." Now you know the consequences on the company, you've discovered the *implication* level of the onion.

Peeling further may result in your customer sharing the implications for him: "I may not have a job."

Now, let's peel the onion one more level deeper, and discover the emotional level. How do the implications make the individuals within that company feel? When your customer confides in you that he/she would feel "really proud" to have helped achieve that increase, and "scared about what might happen" if the increase is not achieved, you will have peeled the onion in a very significant, powerful way. You now understand the customer probably better than any of your competitors because you've focused on understanding the customer's SPOO and PIE.

As always though, the question is, "How do you implement these principles?" The answer? By mastering the single most powerful sales tool available to Six Hat Salespeople.

The Question is the Key

A good sales question is the single most effective tool you can use to bring you the knowledge you need. Stringing together a series of well-designed questions can be your most effective strategy to gain an edge in this most critical part of the sales process. There is simply nothing you can do in a face-to-face interchange with your customer that is more powerful than asking a Good Sales Question (hereafter referred to as a GSQ). Your knowledge of the customer, the depth and nature of your relationship with your customer, his/her perception of your competence, the level of trust developed between your customer and yourself -- all of these are impacted by your ability to create and use GSQs. If you're going to wear the consultant's hat, you <u>must</u> master the competency of asking good sales questions.

THE QUESTION IS THE KEY

Illustration 9-3

A GSQ is your primary means of knowing your customer and collecting information. But it does much more for a Six Hat Salesperson than that. A GSQ functions in several other positive ways.

First, a well-phrased, appropriately-timed question *directs your customer's thinking*. It's almost impossible to be asked a question and not think of the answer. I'm not sure whether it's something in our basic humanity, or if we're conditioned since birth to always think of the answer to a question. To illustrate, I'll ask you a question, but I want

Chapter Nine: The Third Hat – Effective Consultant

you to *not* think of the answer. Here's the question, "How old are you?"

If you're like most of us, you thought of the answer, even after I indicated you shouldn't. That's the point! There is something in all of us that makes us think of the answer when we're asked a question. To not do so takes a steel will and great discipline.

Now, consider where the decision to buy your products or services takes place. Doesn't it happen in the mind of your customer? And the way that you penetrate that mind and get it working in your direction is to ask GSQs. Questions shape the direction in which your customer's mind works.

Here's an illustration. Suppose you're shopping for a new car. The salesperson asks you, "Which is more important to you, good fuel economy, or quick pickup?" Until asked, you hadn't really thought of it that way. The salesperson's question helps you understand what you really think, and directs your mind along a certain course.

So it is with your customers. You can use GSQs to shape and steer the direction of your customer's thinking.

Secondly, a question is a powerful tool to *build relationships* with your customers. Have you ever struck up a conversation with someone in a social setting, and discovered that person was very interested in you? He/she asked about what you did for a living, and showed interest in your hobbies, your family, or your opinions. You left the conversation thinking, "What a nice person!"

What made you like that person? It was the way he/she was interested in you. And how did you know he/she was interested in you? By the questions asked.

The law of reciprocity states that people will respond to you in the way in which you first act to them. That's Dale

Carnegie 101. Show interest in your customer, and he/she will reciprocate by showing interest in you.

The way you show interest in someone is to ask them questions about themselves. You can ask personal questions even if you know the answer. The purpose of the question is not necessarily to get the answer, it's to build a relationship.

In chapter six, we discussed another powerful function of a good question. A series of GSQs *conveys the perception of your competence.* In other words, your prospect sees you as competent and trustworthy -- not necessarily by what you **say** -- but rather by what you **ask**.

There is yet one more function of a good question. This is the one you've been thinking about all along. A good question is your best means of *collecting the information* – understanding the customer and the customers' situation -- that will help you construct a sale. How do you know what a prospect thinks, or what his situation is, unless you ask a question? The question helps you to see what's in the mind and heart of your prospect.

The Six Hat Salesperson knows that a sale is created only after the salesperson thoroughly understands the customer. Often, in a competitive situation, the salesperson who best knows the customer gains the advantage. And the way to acquire that knowledge of the customer is to skillfully use GSQs.

Opening the Sale

One of the best applications for well-constructed, appropriately-timed questions is early in the sales process when you're attempting to peel the onion and uncover the customer's SPOO and PIE.

Remember, the sale often goes not to the person with the best product or price, but to the one who does the best

Chapter Nine: The Third Hat – Effective Consultant

job of understanding the customer. Here's a real life illustration.

I was asked by one of my clients to work with his sales force. The salespeople were having trouble closing the sale. Here's what happened in one sales call I made with one of their salespeople.

We were selling HVAC equipment, and the salesperson had an appointment with the prospect. We met the prospect, and he explained that the building had been added onto several years before, but that nothing had been done to expand the capacity of the air conditioning unit. The company now wanted to do something about that.

The salesperson asked to see the area in question. He measured the square footage of the room, taking detailed notes on a form attached to his clipboard. Then he asked to see the existing equipment. We went up into the attic where it was located, and the salesperson studied the existing unit, estimating the distance from the equipment to the addition.

He ended his information-collecting by saying to the prospect, "I'll fax you a proposal in a couple days. Will that be OK?" The prospect said yes.

At this point, the salesperson had done an adequate job of understanding the technical specifications of the situation, but hadn't even begun to probe into some of the other aspects of the sale. So, I intervened and asked the following questions.

"If you like our proposal, what's the possibility that you'll buy it within the next few weeks?"

Here's what he said: "Oh, none at all. I'm just collecting information for budgeting purposes. We won't actually buy anything until after the new fiscal year in January."

My salesperson didn't know that because he never asked. Instead, he proceeded on the erroneous assumption that the prospect was in a buying mode.

Next I asked about the "situation." I said, "When we met, you said that the addition had been completed a few years ago, but that nothing had been done to upgrade the air conditioning. Tell me, what's changed about your situation? Why is this an issue now?"

He said, "Well, we added space to this building several years ago. It's always been stuffy in the new addition, but we got along OK. At least until last week, when we had a heat wave. The air conditioning had to work so hard that it froze up. So we unplugged it to let the ice thaw. As the ice thawed, it dripped through the acoustical ceiling directly onto the president's desk. So, that's why we've decided to do something about it now!"

Then I said, "What are you looking for in a proposal?"

He said, "Just a ballpark figure we can use for budgeting purposes."

I turned to my salesperson and asked, "What's a rough estimate of what it'll take?"

He responded, "About $3500."

Then I said, "What can we do to make you look good in this process?"

He said, "I just want to get this off my desk. It's an extra project I don't need right now."

I said, "If we get you a ballpark figure, and a set of literature you can show to the boss today, will that help?"

"That would be great," he said.

Finally, I asked, "How will a decision be made?"

"Around here, the president makes all of those kinds of decisions. So, I'll collect the information and give it to him, and he'll decide what to do from there."

"Could we see him?" I asked.

The prospect replied, "Would you?"

"We'd be happy to," I said. At that point, he set an appointment for us to talk to the president.

Let's analyze this experience. Without the use of GSQs, the salesperson would have vainly spent hours preparing and faxing the quote, and then wondering why he didn't close the sale. He was well equipped to respond to the technical specifications, but didn't have the faintest understanding of the customer's gap, and little chance of closing the sale. When we added the skillful use of GSQs, we uncovered the truth of the situation, and positioned ourselves to capture the sale.

The question was the key.

That's how questions can be used to more completely understand the customer as you open the sale.

Questions can be used at every phase of the sales process, but are particularly effective:

* In the initial probing meeting to "open" the sale and understand the customer.
* During your presentation to gather feedback from the customer.
* Following the presentation to achieve agreement on a course of action.

 The Processes

If you're going to become skilled at the use of GSQs, you need to master two processes:

1. Preparing questions word-for-word.
2. Using questions effectively.

✿ Preparing Good Sales Questions

When you're making a presentation, you don't always have to phrase everything you say perfectly. People will understand what you mean even if you're not totally accurate in your choice of words. It's acceptable to say, "About 50%" instead of saying "49.27%."

That, however, is not the case when you're phrasing questions. The language in your question must be perfect, because the words in your question direct your prospect's thinking. A little change in words can make a huge difference in you're prospect's response.

I had created a telemarketing program for one of my clients, and stopped in to follow up with him a couple of months after the program was instituted. "How's it going?" I asked.

"Fine," he said, "the telemarketers are creating lots of leads." "But," he said, "I have a problem."

"What's your problem?" I asked.

"I can't get the salespeople to follow up on the leads," he replied. "So I have a question."

"What's the question?" I asked.

"How can I get the salespeople to follow up on the leads?"

I thought for a moment and replied, " I think that's the wrong question."

"What should I ask?" he said.

"How can I get the leads followed up on?" I responded.

Let's consider what happened. When he asked, "How can I get the salespeople to follow up on the leads," our thinking was directed to the salespeople. The solution to his problem would be limited to salespeople.

However, when we changed the question to, "How can I get the leads followed up on?" we opened up a much larger range of possibilities. Maybe the telemarketers could follow up on them, maybe the owner or sales manager could, maybe the salespeople could, maybe some independent reps could. We opened the door to a world of possible solutions.

You see, the tiny change in wording in the phrasing of the question caused an enormous change in the direction of our thinking, and therefore a major shift in the solutions that followed.

That's why it's important to phrase your key questions word-for-word -- to make certain that they are exactly what you want them to be.

You'll be much more likely to phrase your questions accurately if you spend time preparing them first than if you attempt to do all your composing on the spur of the moment. That's not to say that you'll never create impromptu questions during the interaction with your customer. Of course you will. But you need to have your basic questions prepared before your meeting starts.

By taking the time to prepare questions first, you can be certain that they are the most effective you can make them.

Step One. Frame the situation.

Begin by thinking about the situation you'll be encountering. Take a few moments and construct it in your mind. For example, you may be meeting a new prospect for the first time. Imagine the setting, see the situation, envision the person.

Then think about what you want to accomplish in that situation. In the example, you might have identified these objectives:
* to uncover the prospect's needs and interests
* to qualify him as a potential buyer
* to attempt to set an appointment for a later date
* to begin to create a trusting relationship with him

Now that you have both the situation and your objectives in mind, it's time to begin to develop questions that will take you where you want to go.

Step Two. Brainstorm all the possibilities.

Write down all the questions that you think you might ask. Don't worry about editing them at this point, just get as many questions down on paper as come into your mind. As you create your questions, keep the two basic types in mind -- open-ended and close-ended. An open-ended question is one which can't be answered by one word. It calls for an explanation, and there is no right or wrong answer. A close-ended question is just the opposite -- it calls for a specific bit of information. So, for example, "How do you feel about our proposal?" is an open-ended question, while "Who got the order?" is a close-ended question. Each has a place in the hands of a Six Hat Salesperson.

Step Three. Edit and refine.

After you have created an exhaustive list, go back over it and rewrite those that make the most sense to you. Judge each question by these three rules.

1. *A Good Sales Question doesn't intimidate the customer, imply blame or cause him/her to lose face.*

You may have written this question, "What do you dislike about your current supplier?" Bad question. If the person you're speaking to is the same one who selected that supplier, then you're asking him to admit a mistake he has made. That question implies blame and causes the customer, if he were to answer it honestly, to lose face. Rephrase the question to something like this: "What qualities or behaviors would you really like to see in a supplier?" That question will bring you the same information as the first one, but will do so in a positive, non-threatening way.

    2. *A Good Sales Question prompts the kind of thinking you want.*

Let's say you just presented your proposal. One of the questions you've thought about asking is, "Was there anything in the proposal we didn't address?" That question directs the customer to think about what is wrong with the proposal. Suppose you were to rephrase the question to be "How do you think this proposal will benefit you?" In that case, you've directed the customer to think about the positive aspects of the proposal. When you edit your list of questions, make sure they prompt the kind of thinking you want.

    3. *A Good Sales Question asks for the level of information appropriate to the depth of the relationship.*

As you deepen your relationship with a customer, you can ask deeper questions. Those questions may be totally inappropriate at the onset of a relationship, but perfectly appropriate when you've established some trust and comfort with your customer.

For example, you may want to ask your customer, "How well entrenched is the competition in your organization?" But that question won't prompt an honest answer until you've created a deeper relationship with the customer.

That's why great salespeople are so good at building relationships. Their relationships allow them to know their customers deeper, and that deeper knowledge enables them to present attractive solutions.

Step Four. Develop an effective sequence.

Now that you've edited your questions to the point where each question is as good as you can make it, sort them into the sequence you think will be most effective.

The sequence you use can be almost as important as the language of your questions. For example, you'll almost always want to start at the surface of the onion, asking questions about the most general and superficial subjects, and then gradually work your way into the heart of the onion with more pointed questions.

We'll be discussing sequences in more detail in the next chapter.

After you go through this process of creating good sales questions a few times, you'll find that you're using some questions over and over. Those good, comfortable, questions can be in your tool box as "stock" questions that you can use repetitively.

Some questions that I've found to be particularly effective include: "Tell me about your business." "What's your situation?" "What would have to change for us to do more business with you?"

Step Five. Practice.

Just one more little effort will add the icing to the cake, and take you a long way to becoming a master. Practice the questions once or twice. It'll only take a minute or two of your time. You'll be sure that the phrasing is comfortable for you, and the practice will help plant the questions in your mind.

With that, you're ready to use the single most powerful interpersonal tool in your tool box -- a Good Sales Question.

Chapter Ten:
Effective Consultant – Part II

Using Questions Effectively

You've prepared your major questions word for word. Now it's time to master the process of actually using those questions to understand your customer more effectively.

Here is the process:
1. Set the atmosphere
2. Ask the questions effectively
3. Listen constructively
4. Respond positively.

Step One. Set the atmosphere.

Atmosphere refers to the emotional climate surrounding the interaction between you and your customer. Whether you acknowledge it or not, the customer "feels" something about you and about the time spent with you. The intensity of these feelings varies from person to person and situation to situation, but they are always a part of every sales situation.

Does your customer feel comfortable with you? Are you honest and frank with one another? Is there an atmosphere of trust and respect? Does your customer feel like it's OK to be honest, detailed and thorough communicating to you?

If you could answer "Yes," to all these questions, you'd describe the kind of emotional atmosphere you'd like to enjoy with your customers. Those words describe the kind of emotional atmosphere that is most conducive to having your questions answered thoroughly and honestly.

Whose job is it to create a positive emotional atmosphere between you and your customer? It's yours. After all, you're the salesperson. You're the proactive agent who has a vested interest in achieving a positive outcome to this interaction. Since the outcome (the ultimate sale) is your responsibility, all of the means to that end, including the emotional atmosphere, are also your responsibility. In a world sprinkled with different kinds of customers — older, younger, male, female, pleasant, grumpy, quiet or communicative – it is always your responsibility to fashion a positive emotional climate.

So, how do you create that kind of atmosphere? You apply the principle of reciprocity. This principle states that, **"Generally, people will respond to you the way you first act toward them."**

Reflect a moment and you'll realize that you know this to be true. As with many principles, salespeople, even if they know them, don't always apply them in a disciplined and professional manner.

What happens when you meet someone, and they greet you with a really warm smile? Do you scowl at them? Of course not. You smile back. The principle of reciprocity at work.

Let's say that you come home from a really bad day. Your car broke down, you were tossed out of an account and told never to come back, you lost a sale to your arch competitor, and you stepped in a mud puddle half-way up to your knee. So you come into your home, slam the door shut, throw your briefcase down, and kick the dog out of the way. Does your spouse then say to you, "Oh, honey, so nice to have you home?" I don't think so. Not in my house. What generally happens is that my spouse acts towards me the way I first acted. I become the recipient of some negative emotion – emotion that I initiated.

And on and on it goes. If you want your customers to feel certain feelings when they deal with you, you need to create those feelings by first being what you want your customers to be. If you want your customers to be honest and thorough with you, you must first be honest and thorough with them. If you want them to be comfortable and trusting with you, you must first be comfortable and trusting with them. While it's important that you begin the interaction by modeling the emotion you want to create, it's not an isolated event that applies only to the first few minutes of an interaction. Rather it is the description of your bearing and demeanor throughout every interaction you have with the customer.

Being what you want your customer to be is a necessary first step in the process. Then, when you've begun to influence the emotional atmosphere surrounding the interaction, you're ready to ask your questions.

Step Two. Ask the questions effectively.

Asking questions *effectively* means using good sequences and delivering the questions effectively. Let's look at sequences first.

Imagine a funnel with a large opening at the top and a small one at the bottom. That's an illustration for one type of questioning sequence. It graphically describes the amount of information your question is designed to elicit. The large opening at the top of the funnel indicates a great deal of information prompted by open-ended questions. The funnel narrows, indicating the continuously narrowing, more specific nature of your subsequent questions.

You start with an open-ended question or two, and then slowly narrow the focus of the question down more and more precisely until you're asking very focused questions to collect specific information.

A good application of this technique is in a probing meeting where you are identifying the customer's needs and interests. One specific sequence I call the "1-2-3" sequence.

Start with *one* open-ended question. Then pick *two* topics out of the customer's response to probe more specifically, and ask *three* questions about each of the responses. Using this sequence of questions will almost always present you with an opportunity to present a solution.

Here's an example.

Let's say you're selling production equipment. You begin the funnel questioning sequence with an open-ended question. "John, tell me about the current state of your production line." John tells you about how they've recently expanded to a second shift, that the line has been breaking down more frequently because of the increased wear and tear on the equipment. You decide to probe two areas -- wear and tear on the equipment, and the implication that business is growing because they've gone to two shifts.

You decide to ask three more precise questions about each of those two areas. You say, "It sounds like your business is growing nicely." You pause to turn the statement into a question. John replies, "Yes, we've recently added a major new contract with one of our customers who is doing very well, and three new customers from our representative in the next state."

You phrase your next question. "If things are going that well, are you thinking about investing in upgrading your equipment?" John replies, "Yes, there's talk about it, but we haven't decided what to do yet."

Next, phrase the third question of this sequence. "It might help your decision-making process to have some information about the latest equipment. Should I spend some time with you and the engineer to show you what some of your options are?"

John replies, "Probably wouldn't be a bad idea."

You have just used the funnel sequence, specifically, the 1-2-3 version, to identify an opportunity to present a piece of equipment. It's been my experience that the 1-2-3 sequence, in the hands of a skillful salesperson, almost always uncovers a potential opportunity.

Oh?

One of the most powerful and useful GSQs is the interrogative "Oh?" What happens when you ask someone the question "Oh?" and then pause in silence? Try it. When someone tells you something, say "Oh?" and then be quiet. The person has to jump in and explain. And in that explanation, they give you more information, and generally uncover a deeper layer of truth.

"Oh" occupies a special place in the toolbox of the Six-Hat Salesperson. I believe you can use "Oh" three or four times during the course of a conversation without the person even being aware of it. It's a small and inconspicuous word. And, as soon as you ask it, the person is not thinking about what you just asked, but rather is thinking about what he/she's going to say in response to it. So "Oh" goes unnoticed.

Deeper Layers of Truth

I've named one of the most powerful questioning sequences *deeper layers of truth.* Using it effectively is one of the skills that can mark you as a truly outstanding sales performer. It derives its power from the fact that most salespeople are content to interact with their prospects and customers at superficial levels. They never really take the time or the risk to penetrate deeper than the most superficial conversations. As a result, they're left with a cursory understanding of their prospects and shallow relationships with their customers.

Remember the onion graphic from chapter nine? That analogy also provides a graphic illustration of the concept of *deeper layers of truth.* Imagine your prospects as being like onions. When you deal with them on the surface, you stay on the edge where it's not too pungent, nor too close to the heart of the matter.

While it's easy and safe to remain on the surface and interact with people on only the most superficial levels, it also keeps you away from the heart of the issue where the decisions are really made.

However, some salespeople -- those who want to excel -- develop the ability to penetrate below the surface, to reach the deeper layers of truth. Like cutting into the heart of the onion, they gain the ability to interact with the deeper issues and concerns of their prospects.

Let me illustrate. Suppose you visit a purchasing agent to whom you recently delivered a quote. In the course of the conversation you say something like, "How did we do on that proposal?"

He says, "Not bad, really."

You respond, "Great. When will we know what you're going to do?"

Chapter Ten: Effective Consultant Part II

"We think we'll have it resolved soon," he says.

At this point, most salespeople will leave, thinking that they have collected the most pertinent available information. In fact, they have engaged in a very superficial conversation. They have been held to the outer edge of the onion, and haven't penetrated to deeper levels of truth.

Now, it may be true that the salesperson's quotation was not bad. And it may also be true that the customer thinks they'll have it resolved soon. However neither one of those replies tell the salesperson anything of value. And they don't provide any information on which to attempt to bring the sale to conclusion.

The Six-Hat salesperson will not accept these superficial answers, but will instead direct the conversation to deeper levels.

The technique to do so is incredibly simple. Just ask for further clarification and question your prospect's answer. Use questions like "Oh?" or "What do you mean by...?" Let's see how this works.

Back to the same conversation. When your prospect says, "Not bad," you say, "Oh?" and pause to let him speak. The purchasing agent pauses for a moment and responds, "Yes, you were one of the lowest bids." Now, that's a bit more informative. It's just as true as the statement "Not bad," but it's more detailed, more revealing, and therefore, true on a deeper level. But it's not deep enough. So, you respond, "Does that mean you are seriously considering our proposal?"

"Yes."

"And, is low price the only factor on which the business will be awarded?"

"No. There are a number of other things we're considering."

"What are some of those?"

"Well, obviously, we're concerned about the reputation of the supplier, and the ability to meet our specifications and deadlines."

"And how do you feel about our proposal based on those issues?"

"We are a little concerned about your ability to meet our deadlines."

At this point, the salesperson has penetrated to deeper layers of truth, and is talking with the prospect on a level that can make a real difference. In this instance, the conversation has developed almost to the point of negotiation. As the conversation continues, the salesperson will have excellent information on which to make some important decisions. And, the salesperson will understand exactly where the project is at, and what has to be done to manage the sale to fruition.

Compare that to the first salesperson who was content to accept the first, superficial reply. The second salesperson chose to dig for deeper layers of truth by asking "Oh?" and "Why?" questions and by asking for further or more precise clarification.

This tactic of digging for deeper layers of truth can be used successfully at several points in the sales process.

For example, you can use it when you're probing to discover the prospect's deeper needs and higher priority goals before presenting your product or service.

You may be interviewing a prospect in your first meeting. In response to your answer, he may say, "Yes, we are thinking about upgrading our computer network." Most salespeople will accept that superficially-true answer, and move on from there to say something like, "Good. Can we make a proposal?"

Chapter Ten: Effective Consultant Part II

The salesperson skilled in digging for deeper layers of truth will take the time to understand the prospect more completely and precisely. In so doing, he/she acquires a deeper knowledge of the prospect and, therefore, an edge over the competition. Some questions you could ask in this situation might include these:

"Why are you considering that?"
"What do you hope to gain by the upgrade?"
"What problems are you trying to solve?"
"When, exactly, do you expect to begin and finish this project?"
"Do you have a budget figure in mind?"

Only after digging for deeper layers of truth does the second salesperson move on to the next step in the process. At that point, the salesperson has far better information than the first, and is much better equipped to manage the sale to its successful completion.

At the same time, digging for deeper layers of truth has an additional fringe benefit of causing your prospect to perceive you as competent and professional. As you take the time to intelligently probe the issue, you reveal yourself as a knowledgeable, professional person. The prospect forms an opinion of you based not on what you say, but on what you ask.

In addition, by understanding the prospect more completely and deeply, you become equipped to present a proposal that will more precisely address the deeper concerns of the prospect.

Here are some of the places in the sales process where the deeper layers of truth tactic is most effective:

* in probing for needs and priorities
* to more completely understand a prospect's reactions to presentations and demonstrations

* at closing, to uncover deeper concerns and objections
* to more completely understand the personal as opposed to the business side of a prospect.

Uncovering deeper layers of truth isn't easy. It requires a salesperson to gain skills in asking questions, and to have the courage to hang in when the natural urge is to leave.

Funneling and deeper layers of truth are both questioning sequences that have broad application. You can use them to move your Six Hat sales skills Up-a-Notch. When you've asked your questions effectively, it will be time to implement the next step of the process.

Step Three. Listen constructively.

Remember, one of the primary reasons you ask questions is to stimulate the customer to share information with you. If you're not good at accepting and processing that information, you've wasted the effort that you have expended to get that far. You need to be a good listener.

It many ways, it's more important to listen well than it is to speak well. Remember, you are a consultant. Your value to the customer begins with finding out what your customer wants or needs. You can not discover that information if you don't listen to what your customer says. When your customer speaks, you'd better learn to listen well.

I use the words *listen constructively* very intentionally. When you hear the word *construction* you think of building or assembling something. That's what I mean to imply. It's your job to listen for things to build a relationship upon and to listen for things on which to build a sale.

Chapter Ten: Effective Consultant Part II

One of the best techniques involves programming your mind with some questions beforehand. It's a technique borrowed from speed reading. A speed reader first looks through the book's table of contents, and then asks himself questions about the contents. For example, looking through a book on sales techniques, and finding a chapter titled "The Art of Asking Questions," you might ask yourself, "What good is asking questions?" "What applications do they have in sales?" "How can I use questions?"

Once you've loaded those questions into your subconscious mind, as you skim through the words, your mind seeks out the answers to those questions on a level beneath the conscious.

This technique can work for you by helping you enhance your listening skills. Prior to the sales call, load into your mind the questions you'd like to have answered, and then, as you listen to the customers' responses, your mind will search for the answers to those questions.

Decide what kinds of things you're hoping to hear. Rehearse them in your mind -- create a list. For example, you may say to yourself, before you enter into the interaction, "I want to discover some things Bill does that I can connect with -- things we have in common. And, I want to find out what the company's position is on this new technology, and if there is anything I can do to influence the proposal I made last month that doesn't seem to be getting anywhere."

Now, translate each of those objectives into questions. Your list could then look like this:

"What do I have in common with Bill?"
"What is their position on the new technology?"
"What is their position on my last proposal?

"What would they like to see me change in my proposal in order to get the business?"

At this point, you've loaded into your mind the questions that you can use to construct a more solid relationship and to build a sale. You're prepared to listen constructively.

Listen and observe more than just words. Listen to the subjects your customer chooses to bring up. The things that he chooses to talk about are the things that are the most important to him.

Listen to what is *not* being said. Sometimes people will intentionally talk around a subject that is too emotionally charged for them. For example, a customer may not want to mention the problems he's having with his current supplier if that supplier was his choice. To admit to the problems would be to admit to his mistake.

Finally, notice your prospect's body language. It can reveal a whole dimension of attitudes and feelings that you may not understand any other way.

 Seven Listening Mistakes

 1. *Don't do all the talking.* Too many salespeople talk themselves out of sales by talking too much. The material you use to create a sale is not *your* conversation, it's your customer's conversation. If you're talking, your customer is not. Use the 75/25 rule of thumb. In other words, in every sales interaction, your customer should talk 75% of the time, and you should talk 25% of the time.

 2. *Don't interrupt when others are talking.* First, it's rude. Second, it's unwise. If you interrupt your customer before he's finished, you may never know the things that he was in

the process of telling you. That's a bit of clay for your craftsmanship that you'll never have.

* 3. *Don't start to argue or take exception before the person has finished.* This can be incredibly hard at times. But it's just a variation of the previous rule. It doesn't serve you well to interrupt your customer. It's always better to let him finish.

* 4. *Don't digress with a personal story all the time.* There are times to tell a personal story. It's a good way to connect with your customer, particularly early in a relationship. But it can get tedious if you do it all the time, *and*, you can waste time and divert the conversation if you do it too much.

* 5. *Don't finish sentences for people.* Again, it's rude, and it causes frustration on the part of your customer.

* 6. *Don't wait impatiently for someone to finish so you can interject.* Generally, the person speaking notices your impatience. That can be disconcerting to your customer. If you're fidgeting impatiently while you wait, both you and your customer know that you're not listening to him -- you're thinking about what you want to say in response. You can't listen while you're thinking about your comeback.

* 7. *Don't work too hard at maintaining eye contact.* You'll make people uncomfortable if you use unrelenting eye contact. You need to look away regularly to relieve the tension.

Step Four. Respond positively.

You're not finished when you listen constructively. To be good at asking questions, you need to respond positively to every answer you receive. Don't ask the next question until you have responded to your customer's answer to your previous question.

Your ability to continue to maintain an atmosphere that encourages your customer to answer additional questions rests, in large measure, on your skill in responding positively. And you know that getting your customer to continue to answer questions is an absolute necessity for you to successfully construct a sale.

When you respond to your customer, you send some verbal or non-verbal signal that you are listening and accepting what the customer has said. You don't necessarily have to agree with it, but you must let your customer know that his/her comments have registered with you.

Respond to everything. Every time your customer answers one of your questions, respond to that answer. Make sure that you respond to their answers positively.

You can use body language, like a nod of the head, or a facial expression, like a smile. The important thing is that your customer understands that you have heard and accepted what he has said.

Paraphrasing what your customer says, and feeding it back to him, is a powerful response. Asking a thoughtful question about his answer is another. If nothing else, you can use verbal reinforcers like , "thanks," "really," and "oh" as a response, not as an interrogative.

Once you've responded positively, you're back at the beginning of the cycle – ready to ask your next question.

And when you've asked the questions, gotten the information and therefore gained a deeper and more useful knowledge of your customer, you've acquired the skills to become a master of the third hat, Effective Consultant.

📖 Trying on the Third Hat

The third hat, Effective Consultant, focuses on principles and processes to help you gain a crucial understanding of the customer. The principles are:
1. Your customers want to be understood.
2. Understanding your customer is like peeling an onion.
3. Generally, people will respond to you in the way in which you first acted toward them.

The two key processes are:
* preparing questions
* effectively asking questions.

When you master this set of competencies, and apply them with discipline, your sales performance will take a quantum leap forward. Understanding the customer in depth and detail is 75% of the sales process.

But where do you begin?

Start small, focusing on one type of customer. For example, you may be selling industrial supplies to production supervisors, maintenance supervisors, and, in smaller shops, the owners themselves. Focus on one of those customer types, and work through the "preparing questions" process.

This is another one of those areas where some group brainstorming would be helpful. Talk to your manager about doing this exercise with several of your colleagues. In a brainstorming situation like this, the group will almost always produce better results than individuals working alone.

However, if you can't arrange that, then proceed on your own. Develop that set of questions for one market segment or customer type, and begin to use them. Before every sales call, review the steps in the "using questions effectively" process. Work at improving your ability to set a comfortable atmosphere, probe into the customer's SPOO and PIE, and listen constructively.

As you feel yourself gaining competence in that customer type, repeat the entire process with another customer type. Build on your success, one customer type at a time. Incorporate what you've learned about the customer and about yourself into your preparation for the next customer type.

Eventually, you'll be thoroughly prepared and very competent as you use your mastery of the third hat, Effective Consultant, to understand your customer and distance yourself from the competition.

Using this Hat to Take Your Performance Up-a-Notch

Suppose you improved your competency in this hat to the point where you're one of the best practitioners of the third hat around. What would that look like?

Like this.

You'll be extremely confident in your sales calls, whether you're calling on someone new, or an old customer. That's because you'll have the experience and knowledge of this essential sales competency.

You'll find that this competency closely intertwines with the second hat, Trusted Friend. As you grow in your competency at one of these hats, you'll find your results improving in the other. That's because there is a direct relationship between your customers' trust in you and their willingness to unveil information to you. As you develop the relationship with a customer, that customer shares more information. As that customer shares more information, the relationship grows.

The net result is that you deepen your relationships with your customers as you improve your knowledge of them. A win/win situation for everyone.

You'll discover added confidence in all sorts of interpersonal situations, not just sales interactions. You'll discover that almost always the best approach is to ask questions first. If your child has a problem, if you have a disagreement with a friend, if the boss has an issue to discuss with you -- in almost any situation, you'll discover the power and confidence that comes from asking questions first. As that habit becomes ingrained, you'll find yourself becoming more and more effective in almost every personal interaction.

Finally, you'll watch your sales results almost magically improve. Your customers will respect and trust you, your presentation and proposals will be more focused, and you'll achieve greater results in less time. You will take your performance Up-A-Notch. But, of course you knew that, that's why you've chosen to master the third hat: Effective Consultant.

Chapter Eleven:
Using the Six Hats to Take Your Performance Up-a-Notch

Challenge: One of the highest potential accounts in my territory has a very close relationship with one of my competitors. They are polite to me, but I can't get anywhere.

Although there is nothing new about this situation, it's becoming increasingly common. Think back to chapter one. Remember our discussion of turbulent times? Recall one of the key principles: **Turbulent times impact your customers.**

As a result of the pressures of our transition to the Information Age, your customers have less time and more pressure than in slower times. One natural and common reaction, from their perspective, is to do more and more business with fewer and fewer vendors, and build closer and closer relationships with them. This reduces the time they spend with salespeople, reduces their paperwork and administrative problems, and allows them to enjoy the kind of close relationships it takes in order to shift some of the details and decisions onto their vendors.

That's a great situation if you're one of their chosen vendors. But you may be on the outside looking in, and that's not good.

If you're a new salesperson, or representing a new company, this can be the situation you face most frequently. Almost every account you visit has existing relationships with your competitors. You'd better figure out how to solve this situation or you won't have much of a future.

But you may also be an established salesperson, with existing relationships, who finds your position in an account supplanted by a competitor.

I've been in both these situations.

As a new salesperson for a company that was expanding into a new geographical area, I had almost no business, and my competitors were the vendors of choice in every one of my accounts. Later, as an established representative, I had my largest account announce one day that the company's vice president had signed a prime vendor agreement with my largest competitor, and all of my business was going to be phased out over the next 90 days.

The circumstances surrounding the situation are of little importance, however. The reality is that if you're in this situation, you have a major problem. Your high potential customer is committed, to some degree, to your competitor, and you still must sell in that account. That's a growing information age challenge.

Applying the Hats

Let's start with what not to do. Don't emphasize your Influencer (third hat) skills to continuously press your product/service/offer on your customers. Don't beat them over the head with the superiority of your product/service/offer. Unless, of course, your offering is so clearly superior and so obviously more advantageous to them that someone will risk their job by not buying it from you. If that's the case, then you're probably wise to push your product/service/offer hard. But that is rarely the case.

It is much more likely that the differences between your offer and those of your competitors are probably not as great as they once were – remember, growing 'commodization' is a characteristic of the Information Age.

So, unless you've got a clear, outstanding, job-threatening advantage, don't push your product. In the minds of your customers, the issue isn't the product. To them, the issue is the relationship.

Your customer is sophisticated enough to know that there isn't that much difference between your offering and your competitor's, nor between your service and your competitor's, nor between your prices and your competitor's.

So what do you do?

Put on your first hat (Astute Planner) again. This time, focus on the information-collecting aspect. Dig around the edges of your competitor's business, trying to locate some small and marginal items that you could sell that your competitors don't sell. Don't go head to head with your competitor's strengths; you'll never win. Instead, try to find opportunities that do not infringe on your competitor's business or interfere with his/her relationship in the account. You'll need all the information-collecting skills encompassed in the astute planner hat.

If you're unable to find products that don't interfere with your competitor's relationships, try to find individuals on the margins of the business. Perhaps there are unaddressed departments or areas of the business that have been neglected by your competition. Those are the areas on which to focus. Remember, your primary strategy is to find small, unobtrusive areas to get your product line in without threatening the relationship your competitor has with the customer. If you can find a small place to put your product, you'll create a reason to be in the account, and give yourself an opportunity to build relationships.

At that point, you can put on hats number two (Trusted Friend) and three (Effective Consultant). Use your exposure in the accounts as a reason to build relationships. As you do, you position yourself to be the vendor of choice when and if the competitor stumbles.

Here's another strategy that may fit your account. Use your Trusted Friend hat to identify some individual within the account who is disgruntled with the competition. There is bound to be somebody, some decision-maker or influencer, who will be more comfortable with you than with your competitor. Someone who meshes with you more than the competition. Then use your Effective Consultant skills to identify that individual's SPOO and PIE, and work your product into the account on an individual basis.

One last thought. Sometimes the best thing you can do is maintain a relationship, however superficial, with the key decision-makers. And be patient. I recall being very frustrated with the situation in one of my key accounts where my competitor was firmly entrenched. As I was venting my frustration to my manager, he advised me to be patient, saying that the only thing I could count on was that things would change. My job was to maintain some relationship in the account until something changed. At that point, I'd be positioned to take advantage of that change.

He was right. A year or so later, my competitor changed salespeople and the customer didn't like the new salesperson. The company made some service mistakes, and I had my opportunity. Within a short time, I became the primary vendor.

This is one of the most difficult Information Age selling situations. To be successful, you'll need to skillfully apply a number of hats, while hoping that your competitor never reads this book!

Chapter Twelve:
The Fourth Hat - Skillful Influencer

Welcome to the fourth hat, Skillful Influencer. I realize that some of you, looking at the word "influencer," may have previously thought that this term describes what sales was all about. By now, however, you know that's not the case. Not in the Information Age. Influencing your customer is just one of the six hats, not the whole of the job.

That's not to say that the skills and competencies contained in this hat are unimportant. They are incredibly important. After all, the final measurement of your success is money changing hands. And a major part of bringing that exchange about has to do with your skill at influencing people to do business with you. Without your customers saying "yes" to you in a regular fashion, you're going to soon be without a job. So, you need to concentrate on taking these skills Up-a Notch -- the skills and competencies required to influence people to give you money for what you offer.

In one sense, that's part of the contribution made by several of the other hats. The second hat, Trusted Friend, and the third hat, Effective Consultant, both speak directly to your need to influence your customers. Influence is much easier and more effective when you engage both of those hats. They set the stage and precondition the customer to be receptive to what you're saying. Think of them as necessary but *indirect*.

When you put on this hat, however, you're focusing specifically on your *direct* activity in moving your customer to take action on your behalf.

It's like basketball. At some point, you must put the ball in the basket. But you can't do that without developing the skills of dribbling, rebounding, and passing. Those skills are necessary, but not sufficient. They get you to the point where you have an opportunity to put the ball in the basket. Presenting and closing, the skills we're going to discuss in this chapter, are the equivalent of putting the ball in the basket. And that brings us to the first principle: **Deciding to buy is a process, consisting of a series of small decisions.**

When your customers decide to give you money for what you're offering, that decision doesn't exist in a vacuum. The decision is only the latest in a string of decisions that your customer made along the way.

Let's illustrate with a simple selling situation. Let's say you're selling an expensive product to homeowners – water conditioners. Your company advertises in the phone books, occasionally on TV, and regularly in the newspapers. As a result, you are supplied with a good quantity of leads. When you attempt to sell a water conditioner, it is usually a one-call sales process, with the customers often deciding if they are going to spend money with you while you are there with them. That's about as simple a sales situation as there is. Your own selling situation may be quite a bit more involved than that.

Now, let's look at the process involved, from the customer's perspective, as the customer proceeds to a decision to buy. For a change, we're not going to describe a process for you to follow, but rather one which customers generally follow.

Let's think in terms of the decisions a customer must make along the way. The first decision the customer must make is whether or not to phone your company as a result of the advertisement. If they decide not to, you never hear of them. But some decide to do so, and thus move one step forward in the process.

What's the next decision? One of which you probably haven't thought. They need to decide whether or not to interact honestly with the person on the other end of the phone. Let's say you are in the office and you receive the call. In the first few moments of that call, the customer on the other end of the phone is making a sub-conscious decision as to how candid to be with you. You know that, because you've been in the same position when you've been the buyer. If the person on the other end of the phone is curt, abrasive, a know-it-all, or unconcerned about you, chances are you won't spend a lot of time describing your situation and asking questions. You'll brush if off as best you can, and move on to someone else. So it is with your customers. In this situation, as in yours, they must make a decision to interact honestly with you before the sales process can go forward. That's the second decision in this simple sales process.

Let's start to illustrate these decisions. Look at illustration #12-1 which shows the sequence.

CUSTOMER DECISIONS IN A SIMPLIFIED SALES PROCESS

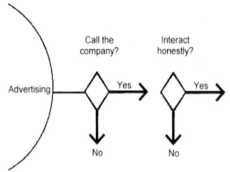

Illustration 12-1

Once they've decided to interact with you, you're probably going to ask for an appointment to see them. The decision to give you an appointment is #3. Our diagram now looks like this (#12-2).

CUSTOMER DECISIONS IN A SIMPLIFIED SALES PROCESS

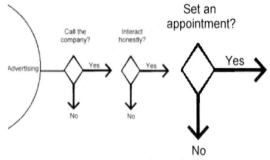

Illustration 12-2

What's the next decision? It's not to buy—you're getting way too far ahead of things. The next decision is whether or not to keep the appointment they made with

Chapter Twelve: The Fourth Hat – Skillful Influencer

you. I'm sure you've had lots of appointments that were broken by one side or the other. It's probably a weekly, if not daily occurrence for some salespeople. If they don't keep the appointment, your time is wasted and your job complicated. So, before you can influence them to spend money with you, you must influence them to keep the appointment. Now, our diagram looks like this (#12-3).

CUSTOMER DECISIONS IN A SIMPLIFIED SALES PROCESS

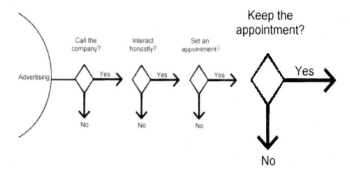

Illustration 12-3

Ok, let's say they have kept the appointment, and you're entering the home of your customers. Both husband and wife are there to talk with you. What's the next decision? It's similar to the decision your customer made in the first few moments of the phone call. They need to decide whether or not to interact honestly and thoroughly with you. If they don't trust you, don't like you, or find something about you that makes them uncomfortable or suspicious, they won't want to deal with you.

In our home remodeling project, we had two electricians come to the house to estimate a significant piece of electrical work. The first was a very personable young man, the owner of a small electrical contracting business who came in the early evening, at the end of his work day.

He was pleasant and knowledgeable, and even offered some ideas on how to do the job less expensively. He took the time to ask some good questions, and got to know our requirements. He said he'd fax me a written estimate the next day, and he did so.

The next day, the second electrician showed up. He called 35 minutes after he was supposed to arrive, saying he was delayed and would be late. He never apologized for being late. When he appeared, he had a bit of a sour attitude about him, and never smiled the whole time he was there. As I showed him the project, he made comments about how difficult it would be. Half way through the conversation, I decided not to spend any more time with him. I never mentioned the complete list of items I wanted done, because I had already decided not to do business with him.

In the first few moments of his time with me, I made the decision not to interact honestly and thoroughly with him.

That's the reality of how your customers operate. Without a positive decision at this point, you'll never have an opportunity to get to the final decision. Our illustration now looks like this: (#12-4).

CUSTOMER DECISIONS IN A SIMPLIFIED SALES PROCESS

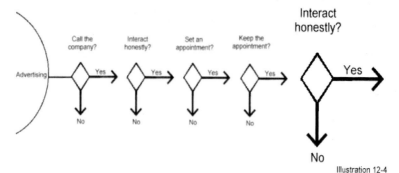

Illustration 12-4

Finally, if you've successfully influenced your customer to make positive decisions along the way, you'll have the opportunity to present them with the final decision, to say yes or no to your offer. (#12-5)

CUSTOMER DECISIONS IN A SIMPLIFIED SALES PROCESS

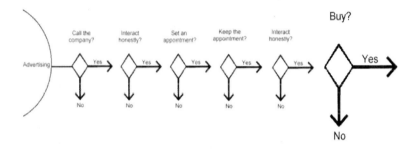

Illustration 12-5

This illustration describes a very simple selling situation. Yet, even in this one-call closing situation, we've identified six specific decisions that customers must make in order for you to walk away with an order. Imagine how complex the process can be to purchase something like a new telephone system that affects almost every employee of the company. Or a major piece of capital equipment around which the production line revolves.

Since this buying process is an involved series of small decisions, you must match it with a process of your own. Your job, as a Skillful Influencer, is to facilitate this buying process so that your customer finds it easy to say "yes" to you at each step along the way. In order to facilitate this, you need to master the fundamental process for influencing people to take action.

📖 Managing an Interactive Sales Dialogue

The heart of the sales process is the conversation with your customers and prospects. It's that moment in time where you are face to face with the customer that defines the uniqueness of your position, and distinguishes you from all the others who work for your company. If you're going to be a skillful influencer, you must master this process.

To begin, let's think about the most basic steps of the sales process. We've looked at a simple sales process from the perspective of the buyer. Now, let's look at a simple sales process, in its simplest form, from the perspective of the seller -- you. What you do when you speak with your customers is this:

* You make them comfortable with you.
* You find out what they want.
* You describe what you offer.
* You show how what you have helps them get what they want.
* You get their agreement to take the next step.

That simple five-step process is basic to every interaction you have with your customer. It's the heart of influencing. It can takes months to complete in an intricate sales process, or it can be whisked through in two minutes over the phone. For example, in the initial phone call from our example above, their decision is twofold: 1) whether to interact honestly and thoroughly with you, and 2) whether to make an appointment with you.

You're job is to facilitate those two decisions. So, you make them comfortable with you, which facilitates the first decision, and then listen to their story, present to them the need for an appointment, and ask for the appointment. That facilitates the next decision. In this short two-to-five minute

Chapter Twelve: The Fourth Hat – Skillful Influencer

phone call, you've progressed through each of the five basic steps.

On a grander scale, let's think about a very complex, long term sales process. Let's say you're selling production equipment with a price tag in the hundreds of thousands of dollars. Several of my clients are in this business. One of them, following my discussion of flow-charting sales processes, identified 27 specific steps to go from the initial meeting to the final resolution of the sale. For the salesperson, each interaction with the customer provides an opportunity to progress through the five steps. But the whole 27 steps can be laid out in relation to the five steps, with each of the 27 specific steps being a small movement toward each of the larger five steps. For example, a salesperson may meet with the production supervisor to get that person's take on the intricacies of the equipment. Then the salesperson may meet with the current operators or foreman to understand their perspectives. Next he may meet with the controller to understand the company's financing preferences and return on investment goals. Finally, the salesperson may meet with the purchasing agent handling the sale to gather that perspective. Those are four specific meetings, four of the 27 steps. Yet they all are a form of step two "Find out what they want." In this case it could take weeks to complete that step.

So, this process is basic to every interaction you have with your customer. It's the heart of influencing.

Let's examine the process and consider how to master it. As you master it, you'll be able to use it effectively countless times throughout the day.

Several years ago, I would have described this process as *making a sales presentation*. But that term emphasizes one-way communication -- you talking to the customer -- and that's just not effective.

So, now I describe this process as *managing a sales interaction*. Here's why I've changed my terminology.

Managing describes your major role. Your primary role is not a presenter of information. Rather, your primary role is to manage the communication process between you and your customer. What happens between you and your customer is solely and entirely *your* responsibility. Like a manager is responsible for the processes in his department, so, too, you are responsible for the communication process between you and your customer.

Interactive refers to the notion that the communication is two-way, not one-way. It consists of conversation between you and your customer. Without conversation from your customer, the sales process is not viable. Selling isn't telling. If anything, the more your customer talks, and the less talking you do, the more effective is the sales call.

Sales refers to the fact that this communication is moving toward an agreement between the two of you. When you're passing the time of day with your spouse, or engaging in light banter at a cocktail party, it's not a sales dialogue. The purpose of the communication is not to come to an agreement. My definition of sales is this: *influencing a customer to come to an agreement with you to purchase something you offer.* The agreement is the main thing. So, this conversation is a sales conversation because it focuses on coming to an agreement.

Finally, it's a *dialogue*. That means it's an honest exchange of feeling, facts, values, and perceptions. The depth and quality of that interaction and communication is the distinguishing standard.

Up-A-Notch
Chapter Twelve: The Fourth Hat – Skillful Influencer

Now, understanding the definition of the process, the question is "How do you manage an interactive sales dialogue so that the chances of its success are enhanced?" Let's start by comparing the process to a baseball game. Illustration # 12-6 graphically describes the process. You know how baseball is played. If you're the batter, you start by taking your position in the on-deck circle. There you wait for your opportunity to get to bat. If you never get to the batter's box, you never have an opportunity to score.

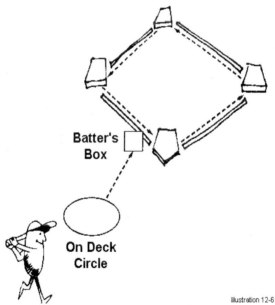

Illustration 12-6

If you're fortunate, you get to the batter's box. Now you have an opportunity to make a hit and score a run. If you're good, and you make a hit, you run to first base. If you successfully negotiate first base, you then move to second base. From second you move to third. At this point, how many runs have you scored?

Obviously, none. Nothing counts until you make it home. Now, let's compare this process to our interactive sales dialogue. Each of the steps in the baseball process corresponds to the four basic steps of the sales process. In baseball, you first need to move from the on-deck circle to the batter's box. Study illustration #12-7.

PROCESS FOR MANAGING AN INTERACTIVE SALES DIALOGUE

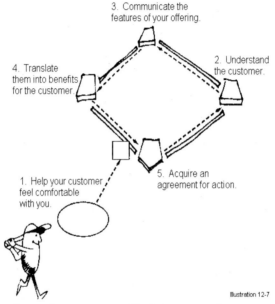

Illustration 12-7

In the sales process, that occurs when you put on your Trusted Friend hat and establish some rapport with the customer and make him/her feel comfortable with you. Without that, you have very little opportunity to go further.

Once you get to the batter's box, you next have to hit the ball and run to first base. First base in the sales process is understanding the customer's needs and interests. You'll use your third hat, Effective Consultant, to do that.

Just like, when you're playing baseball, you can't go to second base until you've made it to first safely, so too, in sales, you can't really talk about your product or services until you successfully understand your customer's needs. You accomplish this primarily by asking good questions, and listening constructively.

Now, you're ready to move to second base. You arrive at second base when you finally earn the opportunity to point out the features of your product or service. From that point you move quickly to third base, which requires you to translate those features into benefits.

Finally, to score a run, you have to safely negotiate home plate. In the sales process, that means that you successfully acquire an agreement from your customer for the next step or the action that both of you will take as a result of your dialogue.

To a great degree, your success as a salesperson will be dependent on your ability to successfully manage interactive sales dialogues over and over again with your customers. Let's discuss each step of this process in detail.

Step One: Get to the batter's box. (Help them feel comfortable with you.)

Getting to the batter's box means that you have created a feeling of comfort and trust in the customer. That's a necessary prerequisite for going further. You don't get a chance to even take a swing unless you've done that.

Here's where you start flipping hats on and off. The techniques we discussed in the sections devoted to the second hat, Trusted Friend, come into play. You employ those competencies in the early part of a sales dialogue to create comfort and interest. Reflecting your customer's style, showing interest, connecting with your customer on a personal and/or business basis – these will be your primary strategies for helping the customer feel comfortable with you.

Step Two: First base. (Understand your customer.)

Once you've achieved that, you can move on to the next step -- getting to first base. In sales, that means understanding the customer. Put on hat number three, Effective Consultant, to achieve this.

This is the time to implement all the skills we discussed in chapters nine and ten. Use them effectively, and you'll do a masterful job of getting to first base.

Step Three: Second base. (Communicate the features of your offering.)

In baseball, once you've gotten to first base, your next goal is second base. So too, in sales, once you've acquired an understanding of your customer, it's time to present your product/service or offering. We'll be discussing this in detail shortly. In the analogy, presenting the features of your offering gets you successfully to second base.

Step Four: Third base. (Translate them into benefits.)

From there, third base is the goal. In sales, that means describing how your product/service/offering will impact the person- your customer. You now talk about the customer, not your offering. We'll discuss this in more detail shortly, also.

In the sales process, you successfully negotiate second and third base by mastering the competency of *presenting*.

Step Five: Home Plate. (Acquire an agreement for action.)

In baseball, nothing really matters until someone crosses home plate. Only then does the score change, and all your effort count. So, too, in sales. Nothing really matters until you get an agreement from the customer to take the next step. The next step could be anything from issuing a purchase order to agreeing to an appointment. The important thing is that your sales process is not successful until your customer agrees to some action.

This requires you to become adept at closing, and that is the issue we'll discuss in the next chapter.

Since we've already discussed the competencies involved in moving from the on-deck circle to the batter's box in previous chapters, let's focus *on presenting and closing,* the two core competencies involved in mastering this hat, Skillful Influencer. These are the skills you use to travel from first base to home plate.

Presenting

Presentations are always about two subjects: your offering and your customer.

One of the most common mistakes that salespeople often make is this—they focus their presentation on their offerings exclusively – forgetting to talk about the customer. It's a common mistake of both the greenest rookie to the most experienced professional. This "product-focused" selling is a vestige of days gone by.

Remember my experience in my first sales training session? Six weeks of memorizing a presentation, all about the features of the product I was selling. That was OK when times were slower, products and services were much more distinguishable from one another, and customers had more time. But no longer.

Today's skillful influencer must do the work for the customer, not only pointing out the features of the product/service, but also translating those into descriptions of how they impact the customer. Skillful presentations are, therefore, just as much about the person (that's the individual, department, or company to whom you're selling) as well as they are about your product/service.

To be effective, you need to sift through all the features of the product/service, select those that are most important, and relate them to the customer. Here's how you do that.

📖 Presenting Your Product/Service/Offering.

 Step One. Describe your best understanding of the customer's objectives.

Here's the best place to start a presentation, although very few salespeople ever do. Why not begin by restating what your customer wants to accomplish? After all, that is what your customer is interested in. It's the reason he/she's allowed you to be there, the reason he/she's invested time in you. Begin your presentation with a restatement of what your customer wants to achieve – the problems to be overcome, or the objectives to be gained. I always prefer to present the customer with a written description of his SPOO, but you may want to do this verbally.

Then, after you have described the customer's SPOO and before you go any further, ask the customer whether you have accurately understood his/her position.

One of two important things will happen at this point. One, the customer may say that "yes," you have understood and accurately described his/her position. That's great. It means that you're beginning the presentation with a positive --- the customer is saying yes to you. Also, you've already distanced yourself from your competitors because you're probably the only salesperson who cares enough to take the

Chapter Twelve: The Fourth Hat – Skillful Influencer

time to make sure you have accurately understood the customer. That will go a long way towards influencing your customer. The customer is impressed that you really do understand.

But what if your customer says "No," you haven't described the situation correctly?

It means one of two things. If you're completely off in your understanding of the customer, then you have no business describing your product/service/offer because it was designed as a solution to your customer's SPOO. If your understanding of the customer is off, your solution will also be off. Stop, encourage your customer to more accurately describe his SPOO, and then make an appointment to come back later with a revised presentation.

It's more likely, however, that you won't have completely misunderstood his SPOO, rather, you'll have missed the mark on one or two small issues. Allow your customer to correct you, thank him/her, and then restate your best understanding of the revised SPOO. If your customer now says, "Yes," then you've achieved this initial agreement, and you can proceed with the presentation.

In either case, you eventually begin with a very positive step that differentiates you from the competition. With that accomplished, you can move into the discussion of what you have to offer as a means of helping your customer accomplish his SPOO.

Step Two. Identify the salient features of your product or service.

Features are describable characteristics of your product/service/offering. For example, if you're selling a mechanical pencil, you could talk about the size of the lead, the weight of the pencil, the color, shape, it's material composition, where and how it was made, it's price, etc. You could also talk about your company's inventory of those pencils, your history, how long you've been in the pencil selling business, how many people have bought them from you. All these are features.

Some are features of the product, but others are features of your company, yourself, and your offering. All of these are part of the buying decision. Your customer doesn't just buy a pencil. He buys it from an individual (you), and a company (your company). He buys it at a certain price with certain delivery arrangements and payments terms. All of these are part of the buying decision and may be described to help the customer make a good decision.

When I'm teaching this module in a sales training session, I'll have the participants pick a product or service they sell, and list ten features. When they're finished, I'll challenge them to double the number of features they've listed. When they're finished with that exercise, I'll often ask them to double, again, the number of features they've listed. It takes some creativity, but it can always be done. The point of the exercise is this – you have far more things to talk about than you have time in which to do so. You can't possibly take the time to describe 40 features of a product, of yourself, of your company and of the offer, so you have to prioritize and only describe those features that are important to your customer.

And how do you know what they are? That's why you run to first base first. You've taken the time to understand your customer's SPOO and PIE, and now you can select those features that are most important to him/her.

Chapter Twelve: The Fourth Hat – Skillful Influencer

 Step Three. Communicate the features with detail and power.

Which of these two statements is more credible?
"It produces about a 50% return."
"It produces 49.67% return."

If you're like most people, the second statement sounds more credible. Why? Because of the detail. There is credibility and substance in accurate detail. Unfortunately, most salespeople are not detail-oriented, so they've fallen into the habits of using general terms, and thereby forfeit much of the power of their presentation. I like to call statements like "...about 50%" as "salesperson's talk." "Salesperson's talk" is comprised of general, vague statements that are difficult to substantiate and designed to be positive-sounding.

Test yourself. If you're buying and you're considering two proposals, which of these two statements makes you feel more comfortable and confident with the salesperson who makes the statements?
"It'll cost around $2,500.00."
"It'll cost $2, 511.27."

There is power in the detail. Use it.

But that's not the only way to add power to your presentation. Another way is to prepare third party recommendations. These can be case studies, letters of recommendation, third party studies, or lists of happy customers. These documents should be designed to support the credibility of what you're saying. Believe me, just because you say it doesn't mean that your customer believes it. If you can provide someone else to support your statement, you'll add power to your presentations.

Here's one other technique to add power to your presentations. Get your customer involved in the presentation as deeply and broadly as possible. If you're presenting a physical thing, for example, hand it to your customer and have them work the latches, flip the buttons, etc. If you're presenting a service or a concept (like an insurance policy) have them fill in the blanks for the calculations, add simple figures, etc. The you're your customers are involved, the more likely they are to believe what they've just encountered, and the more power you've built into the presentation.

Back to the example of the mechanical pencil. In order to add power in the presentation, you may want to hand your customer the pencil and say, "Here, take a look at it yourself." By doing so, you've involved your customer in the presentation, and appealed to a source other than yourself to validate your statement. That source is your customer!

Step Four. Translate the features into specific benefits.

When you translate a feature into a benefit, the subject of your sentence changes. When you're describing a feature, you talk about *it*. When you're describing a benefit, you talk about *your customer*. The subject of a feature sentence is the product or service. The subject of a benefit sentence is your customer.

Remember PIE? Problems/objectives, implications, emotions. Your presentation should parallel those three levels. Features parallels problems/objectives, and benefits parallel implications. In other words, your benefits describe the positive effect your product will have on the implications of the customer.

For example, let's say you're selling that mechanical pencil. You've described the extra long eraser contained inside the top of the pencil. That's the feature. It's a describable characteristic of the thing. Then you translate that feature into a benefit that addresses one of your customer's implications. You say, "This means that you can erase a whole page of notes or a number of columns of numbers without having to change erasers. You won't have to keep separate erasers on your desk, so you'll save money."

That's a benefit. It described the implication on the customer. Notice the subject of the sentence is "You." Here's a simple technique for translating features into benefits. Use the transitional phrase, *"This means that you..."* Because it's a transition, your customer won't even notice the language, yet it helps you stick to the rule of changing the subject of the sentence.

Step Five. Render those into descriptions of positive emotions.

Remember PIE. You've addressed their problems and implications, so now it's time to address the emotional level. Now you're going to render each of the benefits into how that will make the customer feel. Back to the mechanical pencil. You've just said, "This means that you can erase a whole page of notes or a number of columns of numbers without having to change erasers. You won't have to keep separate erasers on your desk, so you'll save money."

Now, you render that benefit into a description of a positive effect on your customer's emotions. You say something like this: "So you won't be frustrated at having to search for extra erasures or aggravated at having to constantly switch from a pencil to an eraser."

And so you proceed through your selection of features, describing the feature, translating it into a benefit and rendering the benefit into a description of a positive emotion.

You can use this inductive approach, or flip-flop the sequence and use a deductive approach, reasoning from the end result, the emotion, to the benefit, and from the benefit to the feature.

 ## Presenting on the Next Level: Concepts and Philosophy

As your customers grow more and more weary of the pressures on them, they look for ways to reduce their stress and ease their time constraints. At some point, with some customers, the issue is no longer which product to buy. Rather, it's which company has the concept or philosophy that most compatibly matches theirs. That is a smart long term strategy on their part.

A great example of this is our own experience with software. I'm sure you have a similar story. A number of years ago, back in the old days of DOS, we had identified a need for a word processing program as well as a flexible data-base. Our search led us to a great software package which was heavily promoted at the time. It was the highest rated world processing program combined with the number one rated data-base program. We bought it, learned to use it, and standardized on it.

It was a great product, perfect for our needs at the time. But, we made a mistake by buying it. A few years later, we watched the growth of Windows-based applications. The company eventually produced Windows versions of both programs, but it was clear they were losing interest in those products, deciding as a company to put their R&D money into other kinds of programs. We were stuck with an obsolete system.

We're smarter now. We've converted to a brand of software that we know is not the best on the market. However, we know the company, philosophically, is committed to continuously improving products for small businesses like mine. Long term, it's going to be less hassle and less time to have gone with a company with a philosophy that's compatible with who we are.

When you're presenting to your customers, think about not just the product or service you offer, but the long-term impact that comes from positioning your company's philosophy.

Regardless, at some point you're going to have completed your presentation, and it will be time to close the sale. And that's what we'll be discussing in the next chapter.

Chapter Thirteen:
Closing the Sale

Let's momentarily review the baseball diamond – the basic influencing process. If you've progressed through the process to this point, you've helped your customer feel comfortable with you -- that's getting to the batter's box. Then, through the skillful use of questions and constructive listening, you have understood the customer's SPOO and PIE. Congratulations.

But, although you may have skillfully accomplished first base and distinguished yourself from your competition in that aspect, you still need to complete the process and run around the bases to score.

You made it around second and third bases by presenting your company, your company's philosophy, your product and service, carefully matching each salient feature to your customer's SPOO and PIE, translating them into benefits, and rendering them into descriptions of positive emotional impact. You've shown your customer why he/she should purchase your product.

Once you complete this step, you've reached third base. At this point, how many runs have you scored? Obviously, the answer is none. Nothing really counts until you have crossed home plate, and that means closing the sale.

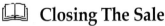 **Closing The Sale**

Whenever I ask salespeople to rate themselves on their competence at all the different parts of the sales process, they invariably rate themselves low at closing the sale. Unfortunately, salespeople who don't resolve the issue and get a decision from the customer waste time. And there is no time to be wasted in the new environment. Being adept at closing the sale, and every step in the process, is an important key to productivity. So, let's examine the issue of closing, beginning with the first principle: **Closing is a process which always ends with your customer's agreement to take action.**

As you consider this principle, you'll realize that closing is not just asking for an order, although it certainly is that. In addition, it is a process you repeat at every stage of the sales process. In fact, almost every time you interact with a customer, you can close the interaction by asking for some agreement. Whenever your customer agrees to take some action, you have closed that step in the sales process.

Let's illustrate this principle with a typical real life situation. Suppose you're talking on the phone to a prospect, and he says, "Sounds interesting. Send me some literature." You say, "OK, I'll put it in the mail today." Have you closed that step of the process?

The answer is no. You have agreed to take action -- send some literature -- but your prospect hasn't agreed to do anything. Remember, a close always ends with your customer agreeing to take some action.

Can you turn the same situation into a close? Back to the same situation. Your prospect says, "Sounds interesting. Send me some literature." You remark, "I'd be happy to. After you review it, will you discuss it with me over the phone, say next Friday?" If your customer says, "Yes," you've closed. He's agreed to take some action.

Understanding this principle is crucial to closing the sale. Many of the offers and proposals on which you work are very involved, requiring a number of steps in the sales process. As you proceed through the sales process, you continually ask for some kind of action in order to keep the project moving forward. When it comes time for the final decision – the agreement to buy -- that decision is often the natural, logical consequence of the decisions that led up to it.

Closing, then, is not an isolated event that only happens at the end of the sales process. Rather, it's a routine part of every sales call. That leads us to the second powerful principle of closing the sale: **Every interaction can and should be closed.** In other words, at the conclusion of *every* interaction with your customer, ask for an agreement on the action he or she will take.

The telephone conversation described above is a good example of closing the interaction. Here's another common situation. Let's say you've discussed a product or proposal with your customer. He says, "It looks interesting, but we're not ready for that now." You might then say, "When do you think will be a good time?" Your customer responds, "Probably around June." You might typically say, "OK, I'll make a note to discuss it with you then." At this point, you haven't closed the interaction, nor have you resolved the issue.

Let's take the conversation one step further. Suppose you now say, "At that point in time, will you spend a half hour with me to discuss it in detail?" You have now attempted to close the interaction by getting an agreement for action on the part of your customer. You've put the issue on the table, and are attempting to resolve it.

Let's take the conversation one step further. Suppose your customer says, "No, probably not." You now have a decision to make. Should you probe the reasons why, or should you accept his decision? Let's say you decide to accept his decision. The conversation has value to you in that you learned that this proposal isn't going to fly in this account. The early "no" was valuable to you. You didn't waste months chasing something that wasn't going to happen. That's the value in resolving the issue.

Let's now say that your prospect, instead of responding "no," responds to your close by saying, "Yeah, I think it has enough merit to spend that time discussing it with you." You now have his commitment to spend some time with you, so you have moved the issue forward. You're one step closer to the ultimate sale.

Implement these two principles and you'll dramatically improve your productivity. Keep in mind that closing is an agreement for action on the part of your customer, and make it your goal to close every interaction.

The Closing Process

Closing is, at least on the surface, a simple two or three-step process:
- * Ask for action.
- * Respond appropriately.
- * If necessary, ask again.

In order to take the mystery out of the process and make it more comfortable for everyone, we're going to diagram the process in more detail. Study illustration #13-1, which illustrates the dynamics of the closing process.

Up-A-Notch
Chapter Thirteen: Closing the Sale

THE DYNAMICS OF THE CLOSING PROCESS

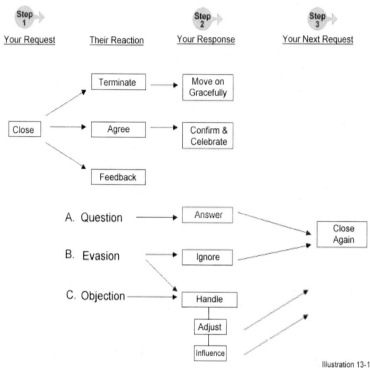

Illustration 13-1

🏃 Step One. Ask for action.

The closing process begins when you ask your customer for some action. If you never put the issue on the table and ask for some action, you'll never close the sale. Certainly some customers will close the sale, and some sales will close in spite of you. But you won't close them.

So, the process begins when you ask your customer to take action. That's the close. When you make a request, your prospect then reacts to your request. There are only a limited number of ways in which your customer can react. As the illustration shows, your customer can terminate, agree, or offer feedback. By definition, everything he/she says can be fit into one of those three categories. Let's look at each.

He can terminate the conversation by telling you definitely, absolutely, without question, "NO!" I call that the terminal no. Or, he can respond with a tentative "no."

It's very important for you to be able to distinguish a terminal no from a tentative no. A tentative no is when the customer says "no," but really means something like, "probably not," or "maybe."

I recall one of my most memorable illustrations of this principle. It was my first visit to an account that had been assigned to me. I was able to meet with the Materials Manager -- a crusty older man who delighted in making salespeople squirm. I did my introductory pitch to him, and he responded with this comment: "Young man, we have too many vendors right now. We're trying to reduce the number of vendors we have. So we're not interested in dealing with someone new. Secondly, we don't know much about your company. But what we do know, we don't like. So, I'd advise you to not waste your time here."

I interpreted that as a tentative no, not a terminal no. Several weeks later I went back to see him again. This time, I thought I'd play my strongest card by presenting a product which almost every hospital in the state bought from us -- suction tubing. Suction tubing is a staple item in a hospital, and is used by every hospital in a number of different departments. At the time, we had an arrangement with the premier manufacturer guaranteeing us the best prices in the state. Almost every other hospital bought it from us. I was sure he had to buy my suction tubing deal.

After I presented it to him, he sighed and said, "We don't use any." I turned in my chair and looked into the hallway outside his office. There was a cart with some suction tubing hanging from it. Telling me they didn't use suction tubing was like saying they have no beds in their hospital. He was lying -- I knew it and he knew it.

I chose to interpret that as a tentative no, not a terminal no. As luck would have it, several months later, I was able to find a buyer in the hospital with whom I could work. I discovered a tiny opening when one of their current suppliers let them down, and I was given an opportunity to bring in a product. We did well with that line, and one thing led to another. Within three years, that account had grown so much that it became the hospital in which I had the greatest penetration of all my accounts. All because I was able to distinguish between a tentative no and a terminal no.

Of course, there's always the possibility that your customer will agree to your request. Good for you. When your customer agrees to take some action, you've closed! Enjoy it.

The most common response, however, is to offer some feedback. There are only three kinds of feedback. By definition, every possible word out of their mouths will fit into one of these three categories: question, evasion, or objection.

You know what a question is. An evasion is when your prospect makes a comment that suggests he isn't willing to commit himself to any position. The classic, "I want to think about it," is an example. An objection is a reason for not doing what you want your prospect to do. Once your prospect has reacted, it's time for you to respond to his reaction.

Step Two. Respond appropriately.

Let's think about each of these possibilities. If he terminates, what is your most appropriate response? Move on gracefully. Don't get angry, don't slam the door or call him names. You never know when that person will surface again at some other account. Move on gracefully, remembering the first law of sales: you don't sell them all.

If he agrees, confirm the agreement and then celebrate! Good for you, you got one. Enjoy the burst of pleasure that gives you. It's one of the reasons you're a salesperson. There is a certain satisfaction and a high that comes from getting agreement, especially on a big deal, that is a special fringe benefit of selling.

Let's look at feedback. If your customer asks you a question, what do you do? Answer the question. That's simple enough.

If he evades your question, you have two appropriate choices. The first is to ignore his evasive comment. That's right, ignore it. I remember hearing a sales trainer some years ago talk about ignoring a customer's first evasion. He said that the first time someone offers you an evasion, they are merely processing the issue in their mind and don't really mean what they said. So, it's often best to ignore it and go on.

Let's say you ask the question, "Should we go ahead with this?" And your prospect says, "I'd like to think about it a little." Your response is, "Should we deliver it Monday, or is Tuesday better?" You've totally ignored their comment.

I have found this technique works once -- for their first evasion. But don't do it more than once in an interaction.

Your other choice is to handle your customer's objection.

Up-A-Notch
Chapter Thirteen: Closing the Sale

 Handling Objections

Now you're dealing with an objection – a reason to say no. It should come as no surprise to you that the best way to handle an objection is with a process. Here it is.

 Step One. Empathize.

Begin by empathizing with your customer. That takes some of the tension out of the situation, defuses any defensiveness on his part, and builds a positive atmosphere. Empathizing requires you to do two things. First, make a statement indicating that you understand how the prospect thinks or feels. Second, support that statement with some proof.

Here's an example. Let's say your prospect has said, "I want to think it over." You respond by empathizing. You say, "I know how you feel," (that's your empathizing statement). "Many of my other customers responded the same way when they were first presented with this concept," (that's your proof). Your proof is the reason they should believe that you really do understand how they think or feel.

 Step Two. Probe.

Once you've empathized with your customer, then ask questions. Generally, when you're responding to an objection or evasion, the issue is too general to deal with effectively. Often your customer hasn't accurately articulated the thoughts in his own mind. Your questions, therefore, should be of the type that requires your customer to think more specifically. You must take his answer from the vague and general to the specific. You can't respond to a vague comment, but you can respond to a specific one. The primary tool for moving your prospect from general to specific thoughts is a good question.

Back to our example. After you've empathized, next ask, "When you say that you want to think about it, what specifically is it that you need to consider more deeply?"

Notice the question asks the prospect to think more specifically -- to move from the general to the specific.

Step Three. Verify.

When he answers, you then rephrase the answer and feed it back to him, confirming that it really is the way he thinks or feels. Back to the example. Let's say he says, "Well, John, I'm not sure about the price. It's more than we had planned in the budget. I'm not sure we want to pay that much." That would be a great answer, because it reveals the specific issue that is bothering the prospect.

Your skillful empathizing and questioning has uncovered the real problem. Now, you just rephrase it and ask for him to confirm what you've said. Your response could go like this. "OK. So, in other words, you're concerned about how you can pay for it when it's more than what you had budgeted. Is that right?" When your prospect confirms it, you have successfully probed and clarified his evasion or objection to the point where you've moved from the general to the specific. Now, you can deal with it.

As long as he maintains that he "just wants to think about it," there is little you can do to move the project forward. But now that you understand exactly what the issue is, you can respond to the objection.

Step Four. Respond.

OK, you've clarified your prospect's evasion or objection to the point that it's a specific, understandable issue. Now what?

You respond in one of two ways. Your first option is to adjust your proposal or presentation to your improved understanding of your prospect's situation and perception. In other words, you change. If your prospect says, "It's two dollars too much," then you have the choice of saying, "OK, for you, we'll drop the price by two dollars." You've changed your proposal to meet your revised understanding of your prospect.

Your second option is to respond to the objection in such a way so as to influence your prospect to change. That means that you must get him to think differently.

How you do this can vary tremendously by the type of objection your prospect has raised. There are an unlimited number of objections, and an unlimited number of ways to respond to them. Rather than attempt to identify a hundred different strategies, I'd prefer to show you a process you can use to create your own responses.

Process for Preparing to Handle Objections.

The secret is to *prepare* for your most likely objections. Remember the principle behind the Astute Planner hat: *You'll always be more effective if you think about what you do before you do it.* That principle applies here, also. In order to do so, use this process.

 Step One. Identify the most common objections you hear.

For any product or service you offer, there are five or six objections that will form the bulk of every objection you hear. If you can anticipate what those objections will be, you'll complete step one of the process.

❦ Step Two. Outline a response.

Having identified each of the most common objections, you now think about the most effective way to respond when you do hear them.

Here's an example. Let's say your prospect says, after you have probed and clarified his first response, "It costs too much." As you think about responding to this objection, you decide that the first thing you're going to do is empathize once again.

So, you put a number one on your outline and write in "Empathize." Then what? You decide you need to find out how much is too much. So, you pencil in a number two, and write, "Ask how much is too much."

Next, you decide to restate the benefits of your proposal to the customer. So, you write number three and note, "Restate the benefits." Then you decide to translate the too much amount into the smallest way of expressing it. In other words, if it's $500 too much, and that is for a year-long time period, then it's really only about $1.35 a day too much. So, item number four becomes, "Translate into lowest expression."

Next, compare the benefits to that low expression. So write down next to number five, "Compare benefits to lowest expression." Finally, you decide to close again -- that goes on the last line of our outline.

Now, what you have is an outline of the steps you want to follow when you hear this objection. But you're not finished yet.

❦ Step Three. Acquire your ammunition.

Gather the ammunition you'll need to support your position. Ammunition is anything you can use to support your statements. For example, do you have any third party

Up-A-Notch
Chapter Thirteen: Closing the Sale

studies that confirm the benefits you've described? Any testimonials, articles from trade journals, etc.? That's all ammunition. Gather that kind of documentation, and have it in your briefcase ready to use when you meet your prospect's objections.

That brings us to the last column in Illustration #13-1, and the last step of our larger closing process.

Step Four. Close again.

"Close again" means that, after you have responded to your customer's statement, you once again make a request for your customer's action. That starts the whole process all over again.

Team Decisions

How do you close the sale when the decision is made by a team or committee, and you can't be there when they make the decision?

This situation is growing more and more common as the trend towards Total Quality Management programs spreads and teams do more of the decision making that was previously the job of individuals. In closing this situation, I'm going to first assume that you've done a thorough job of selling. In other words, you have reached all the available team members, talked with them individually, understood their SPOO and PIE, and made a coherent, powerful presentation of your best solution to their problems and objectives. If you haven't done that, then you need to do it first, before you attempt to bring the issue to closure.

Now, let's say that you have finished selling, and the team is going to make a decision. What do you do? Here's the most effective approach. Find the team member who you think is most strongly in favor of your solution, and ask him or her to advocate it to the team. Your request for action is not, "Will you buy this?" Rather, the issue you put before that team member is, "Will you recommend this?"

If you can get one strong team member who is on your side and willing to argue for you, your chances of closing that sale will be dramatically enhanced.

Alternate Next Steps

Much of the literature about closing works on the assumption that the person to whom you're speaking is the decision maker, and that he has the authority to make the decision while you're there with him/her. However, this situation is growing increasingly less frequent. Many organizations are adopting policies and procedures that require multiple sign-offs on a decision and/or team approaches. In such cases, it's inappropriate for you to ask for the order when your prospect does not have the appropriate authority.

In this situation, it's important that you develop alternate next steps. While you may want the purchase order, your buyer may not be able to give it to you for reasons that are totally beyond your ability to influence. Your best strategy is to back off, and ask for something that isn't quite as difficult. I call that *preparing an alternate next step*.

Here's an example. I once had a CPA firm as a client. The firm wanted to acquire additional customers for its computerized bookkeeping service. We developed a sales and marketing system which put them in front of a number of qualified prospects. At the first sales call, they asked the prospect to sign up for their bookkeeping service.

Think back to the discussion of risk and relationship from chapter six. Giving someone your bookkeeping business is a high risk decision. Few prospects are ready to do that on the strength of just one sales call. So, when it became apparent that someone was not going to say yes to the major proposal, they were prepared with a fall-back position. The fall-back position was to ask the prospect for a set of their financial statements, so that the CPA firm could prepare an example of what the computerized report would look like, using their own figures.

Notice that this *alternate next step* kept the proposal alive and moving forward while at the same time recognizing that some people were legitimately not ready to say yes to the big deal.

That's an example of an alternate next step. One of the best ways to prepare for closing is to think through each of your closing situations, and to prepare one or two alternate next steps that allow your prospect or customer to say yes to you and keep the project moving forward.

Master these processes and you'll gain the magic of the fourth hat: Skillful Influencer.

Trying on the Fourth Hat

I know. The task of acquiring the magic of the fourth hat may seem overwhelming. After all, there were four powerful principles:
1. Deciding to buy is a process, consisting of a series of small decisions.
2. Presentations are always about two subjects: your offering and your customer.
3. Closing is a process which always ends with your customer's agreement to take action.
4. Every interaction can and should be closed.

These are some of the most powerful and useful principles for a Six Hat Salesperson, addressing the very

heart of the salesperson's job. In addition, this hat contains some of the most frequently used and most intricate processes. They were:
* the "managing an interactive sales dialogue" process
* the presentation process
* the closing process
* the handling objections process
* preparing to handle objections process.

It's no wonder you may be feeling a bit overwhelmed. As always, however, you can make the magic of the fourth hat yours by taking one small step at a time, and by building on your successes.

So, where do you start? At the end, with closing. Learn two all-purposes closing questions.

"Where do we go from here?"

"What's the next step?"

Then use one of those closes at the end of every interaction with a customer. It may be a phone call, an information- collecting call, a service call – it doesn't matter. Just discipline yourself to the habit of asking for an agreement for action at the end of every conversation.

You'll be amazed at what this little change will do for you. You'll find yourself pushing projects forward that would have otherwise been stalled. You'll also find yourself resolving issues and moving on when before those issues would have been left simmering on the back burner for months. Later, as you gain confidence in that simple closing technique, you can build on your success and develop more sophisticated closes.

As soon as you achieve some comfort with the closing question, focus on your presentations. Take some time and think about a presentation that you're scheduled to make.

Rearrange it so that it fits the presentation process described earlier. Then practice it a time or two so that you're comfortable with it, and try it out.

This is another one of those issues where a group approach may be of more benefit to you. Suggest a group brainstorming session to your manager. If you can arrange that, great. If not, push forward on your own.

As you become comfortable with the format for one product, spend that same amount of preparation time on all of your other products and services, moving from those most commonly presented first to those least commonly presented last. Eventually you'll find the presentation process to be second nature to you.

At that point, you'll be well on your way to mastering the fourth hat: Skillful Influencer.

Wearing the Hat

So what happens when you've mastered this hat to the point that these principles, processes and tools are habits, and you don't need to think about them anymore?

Your sales dollars per opportunity identified will dramatically improve. You'll be known throughout your company as the salesperson who wrings more dollars of an account that anyone else. And it's easy to understand why that will be.

You'll be more effective on every contact you have with your customers, turning almost every conversation into a step in a constantly moving positive process. As a result of your penchant for moving projects forward, your customers will come to respect and rely on you more, because they know that things seem to get done when you're involved.

You will have practiced and used the presentation process so often that you won't have to think about it any more – it'll be routine. But, every now and then, you'll take the time to analyze your presentation for a new product, program or service to make sure that you're continuing to adhere to the process and not getting sloppy.

Every time your company develops a new product or service to sell, you'll organize the presentation in terms of the baseball diamond analogy, and practice making a presentation.

For every new offering, you'll also spend a couple of hours working through the process for preparing to handle objections. That work will pay dividends to you in multiples. In fact, you'll be closing at a far better rate than anyone else.

The confidence that brings you will spill over into every aspect of your job. All because you've truly become a master of the fourth hat: Skillful Influencer. You will have taken your performance up-a-notch.

Chapter Fourteen:
Using the Six Hats to Take Your Performance Up-A-Notch

Challenge: My customers are confused because they have more choices than ever before. It's difficult to get them to make a decision.

Reflect for a moment on the first chapter, where we discussed "Turbulent Times." It's easy to see why this is a commonly occurring phenomena of the Information Age. In the same way that the whitewater in a river is the most superficial indication of the rocks that lie beneath the surface, so this confusion is the symptom of some of the trends that lie beneath the surface.

As more and more information becomes available, our customers become overwhelmed and confused by it. Technology creates new options, and new competitors spring up, vying for their business. Should they search the internet for your product or service, respond to the people who are sending them catalogues in the mail, try that new competitor who is calling on them all the time, or stick to their old standby? No wonder they are confused.

And then, of course, there is the complexity and change on the inside of their businesses. It often seems like their own needs and applications are a moving target. They might need a new piece of equipment to assist in the production of a product today, but what if that product changes tomorrow? Can you blame them for hesitating about making a decision?

As always, your customer's confusion and uncertainty provide both an obstacle as well as an opportunity for you. It's an obstacle because it causes them to be uncertain and hesitant in making a decision. It's an opportunity because they are just as uncertain and confused about your competitor's offer as they are about yours. If you can figure out how to help them make those decisions, you'll gain a significant competitive edge.

Applying the Hats

You can use two hats to effectively handle this challenge – the second hat, Trusted Friend, and the third hat, Effective Consultant.

Let me illustrate from my own experience as a buyer. In my business, we have a continuously changing need for graphic design services, as well as for audio and video production services. I'm regularly revising our promotional materials to meet the changing requirements of a constantly morphing market. What looks good and is right today may be hopelessly obsolete in just a few weeks or months. So, at any one point in time, I'm very hesitant to say yes to a new brochure or graphic design. It could be obsolete momentarily.

I've solved this headache by developing a relationship with a graphic designer who is responsive to all our changes, and sensitive to our time needs. So, if we do want to change a design or a brochure three weeks after we last changed it, we can count on the relationship with the designer to easily facilitate those changes. The relationship is more important than any one particular design.

Chapter Fourteen: Using the Six Hat to Take Your Performance Up-A-Notch

Sure, we could probably entertain a dozen proposals from a dozen different designers for each project. And certainly the chances are slim that our regular designer will have the outstanding design for each of these projects. Odds would be 11 to 1 against him.

But that's not the point. The relationship, the ability to change and be sensitive to our needs and keep us up to date on the latest techniques and methods, is far more important than any one design. Over a period of time, we're far better off building a working relationship with a competent person we can trust than we are taking any other course.

As a seller, when you find a customer who is hesitant to make a decision, it may very well be because you're focusing on the product or service you're offering, and your customers are concerned about the likelihood of an ongoing relationship.

Or what about our needs for audio and video production? We have a need to regularly create multi-media training products. Sometimes these are video projects, sometimes they're audio, and sometimes there are combinations. Sometimes they are done for our own product catalogue, and sometimes they are produced under contract specifically for a client.

Again, we could put each of these projects out for proposals. Our area is full of audio and video producers. We could probably get a dozen people to develop proposals for us. And, the likelihood of our regular suppliers always having the outstanding proposal is small. But, the ongoing relationship is more important than the individual proposal.

From our perspective as a buyer, life is easier if we can work with a competent person we can trust. While we understand that every project may not be the absolute most creative and outstanding, we also understand that the body of work will certainly match anyone's standards.

More important than any one project is the ability to easily communicate and trust people who will be responsive to our needs and capable of changing to meet them.

All of the above are reflections of my motivations as a buyer. My motivations and concerns are similar to your customers. As we are swept along by the turbulent tides of our entry into the information age, it's more and more important to find anchors upon which we can rely. In a buyer-seller context, those anchors can be relationships.

The moral of the story? Take seriously the principles and process involved in the second hat, Trusted Friend, and build solid relationships with your key customers. Help them to see you and your company as "competent people they can trust." If the relationship is intact, the decision becomes easy. Remember our discussion of risk and relationship? The greater the relationship you have with your customer, the less is the perceived risk in the minds of the customer. Build solid relationships, and they'll make decisions more quickly.

That's the first line of attack. At the same time you are relationship building, work at bringing value to your customers by implementing the third hat, Effective Consultant. Pay particular attention to knowing your customers by peeling the onion. The deeper is your understanding of your customers' situations, their SPOO and PIE, the more likely it is that you'll present them with proposals that will be easy for them to resolve. When decisions are difficult for your customer, it is often because there is some unknown variable. If you do the best job of understanding your customers' SPOO and PIE, and the best job of presenting solutions to your customers, your

Chapter Fourteen: Using the Six Hat to Take Your Performance Up-A-Notch

proposals will make it easier for them to make decisions. You will have most thoroughly addressed all your customers' concerns.

★ The issue isn't what you do, it's how well you do it. Distinguish yourself from your competition by being better than anyone else at implementing the second and third hat competencies, and you'll find your customers making decisions easier and quicker. You will have taken your performance up a notch.

Chapter Fifteen:
The Fifth Hat – Adept Human Resource Manager

 The position of human resource manager came into prominence in the decades of 1980's and 90's as companies began to understand that one of their greatest assets was the group of human beings who worked for them – their employees. That realization coincided with the spread of the human potential movement, which proclaimed belief in the untapped, limitless potential of human beings. Hundreds of books and articles were, and continue to be, written to urge the readers to greater heights of achievement. Motivational speakers now criss-cross the world, urging their audiences to tap into their potential to achieve success.

 It's not difficult to see how these two trends intersect. If human beings have the huge untapped potential for success and achievement claimed by the motivators, then the wise company will develop a climate where the unleashing of that potential can take place. It's to the company's benefit. And a human resource director is often the executive in charge of maximizing the company's human resources.

 "So," you're thinking, "What does this have to do with sales, or with me?"

 This. If you're a human being, you have a vast reservoir of untapped potential. If you can learn how to unleash more of that potential, your career will soar. So,

Chapter Fifteen: The Fifth Hat – Adept Human Resource Manager

who is in charge of managing you in such a way as to unleash your potential? You've got it! You are!

Welcome to the fifth hat, Human Resource Manager. The human resource you manage is *you*. When you put on this hat, you work with principles and processes to unleash your potential, so that you're working at continuously increasing levels of effectiveness.

It took me about six months in my first full time professional selling position to realize that much of my challenge as a salesperson resided inside my head, not out in the external world. Like the average outside salesperson, I spent only about 1/3 of my work week actually face to face with customers. That's probably true of you, too. So, with whom do you spend the rest of your time? More than anyone else, with yourself. Which means that if you are going to be successful in the Information Age, you must learn to get along with yourself. You must learn how to unleash your potential, maximize your human assets, and eliminate the obstacles that hinder your performance.

Unleashing your potential, overcoming adversity, dealing with procrastination, handling rejection and depression – these are the internal issues that can seriously impact your performance. It doesn't matter how smoothly you interact with your customers if you can't manage yourself.

To become a maser of this hat, you'll need to master positive, proactive principles that help you unleash your potential, as well as principles that help you overcome those negative hindrances that drag down your performance. Here's the first: **You are always more effective when you set goals.**

One of the most effective strategies to get the most out of yourself is to master the discipline of regularly setting

Chapter Fifteen: The Fifth Hat - Adept Human Resource Manager

powerful, motivating goals. Goals compel you to work with discipline and focus rather than going about your job mindlessly and routinely.

This doesn't mean that you can't do your job without goals. You can, and many salespeople do. But the discipline of goal setting forces you to think about what you do before you do it. It moves you out of the realm of being reactive -- doing what other people want you to do -- to being proactive -- doing what you want to do.

It provides focus and direction to your activities, and supplies the motivation to push yourself beyond your comfort level. For example, if you're producing at about a rate that provides you a comfortable living, you may be content with your situation. Since you're content, you probably aren't going to grow and change because there is no reason to do so. However, if you commit to a goal of "Increasing my business and therefore my income by 20%," then you've got to stretch yourself out of your current patterns of behavior to reach that goal. The goal is the device that prompts you to stretch yourself and to focus your efforts.

Goal setting is the beginning point in taking control of your job (and, in the same way, in taking control of your life). It is possible to go about your job in a purely reactive way. You can visit all your customers on a route-type basis, taking care of their problems and responding to their issues. Your day is determined, not so much by what you want to accomplish, but rather by the problems and demands of your customers.

Look at Illustration # 15-1. It depicts a spectrum which describes the styles of doing your job.

Chapter Fifteen: The Fifth Hat - Adept Human Resource Manager

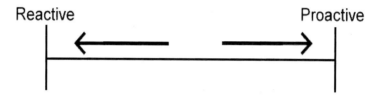

Illustration 15-1

At the far left end of the spectrum is the purely reactive style. The person who is purely reactive starts the day with no plan other than to see that day's customers in reply to that day's inquiries. He has no sales goals -- seeking only to respond to what his customers ask for. He mindlessly goes through his days, weeks, months, and years responding only to other people's requests.

On the far right is the salesperson who is so proactive that he/she refuses to return phone calls if they aren't on the agenda.

While straying too close to either end of the spectrum can be a problem, it's been my experience that most salespeople tend to cluster on the reactive end of the spectrum. As a result, they are not nearly as effective as they could be.

If you look at the spectrum, it's obvious that the fundamental difference between the salespeople on the left and those on the right is the presence of goals. You can't be proactive and work your agenda unless you have an agenda. An agenda is a plan to achieve some end. And that end is a goal. So, an agenda begins with a powerful set of goals. The first step, then, in moving from reactive to proactive, is to create a set of goals.

If you want to become an effective human resource manager, wringing the most out of yourself, a powerful set of motivating goals is the starting point.

Chapter Fifteen: The Fifth Hat – Adept Human Resource Manager

Goal-setting is much more than just an occasional exercise. Rather, it's a disciplined way of thinking about your job and your life that takes you from being reactive to becoming proactive. Think of it as a mind-set, not a task.

You'll need to build it into your life on a regular basis. Every year or so, review and refine your long-term (lifetime) goals and create a set of annual goals. Every few months, review your short-term goals. Regularly create monthly, weekly and daily goals.

Regardless of what level you're working on, the process is always the same. Here are the steps you need to master to become an effective goal setter.

The Goal Setting Process

 Step One. Select an area on which to concentrate.

This can range from the very deep and foundational, to the very specific and superficial. For example, you may want to focus on something like your spiritual growth. That's a deep and foundational area. Or, you may want to focus on something much more specific, like the state of repair of your home. Regardless, you must begin by selecting an area of your life or your job on which to focus.

 Step Two. Select the time period.

There are lifetime goals that give purpose and definition to your life. Then, there are long-term goals, which are eight to twelve years from now. Mid-term goals address the time period from one to eight years in the future. Short-term goals can be anything from a week to a year.

Let's say that you want to work on annual goals for the financial aspect of your life. You've now identified the area (financial) and the time period (annual). You're now ready for the next step.

Step Three. Brainstorm (daydream) to create a list.

Now, you're going to create a long list of possibilities. You do this by looking at both the "gain" and the "pain" in the area you've selected. "Gain" means the positive things that you'd like to have, while "pain" means focusing on the negative things of which you would like to be rid.

To focus on the "gain," daydream about what you'd like to achieve with respect to that part of your life. Kick back, relax, and begin to list on a piece of paper all the things you'd like to accomplish in the area in which you're working. Ask yourself these three questions:

- What would I like to be?
- What would I like to do?
- What would I like to have?

Create a list of your dreams. Don't edit or judge what you've written, rather, just make a long list of your dreams. No one else can do this for you because no one really knows your situation and your aspirations better than you do.

Let's say you write these things down:

"Make a lot more money"
"Buy a new car"
"Put aside $2,000 in a retirement account"
"Save some money for the children's education"

You've created a list of possible annual goals for the financial aspect of your life.

Now, look at the "pain" side of the issue. What problems do you have that you'd like to solve? Make a list.

Then select from that list one or two with which to start. Let's say, for example, that your list contains these two sales problems that you want to solve: "Stop wasting time," and "Stop losing potential new accounts to competitors."

Let's turn these problems into goals or objectives. It's easy. Just rewrite each problem as an objective, beginning with the word "to." So, "stop wasting time" becomes "To stop my wasting time," and "Stop losing potential new accounts to a competitor" becomes "To stop losing potential new accounts to competitors."

Now, let's work with these statements in one more way. Let's turn the negative statement into a positive statement. So, instead of saying "I want to stop wasting time," say, "I want to make better use of my time." And, instead of saying, "I want to stop losing potential new accounts to competitors" say, "I want to gain new accounts."

It's amazing what this little change in language can do for you. Human beings are made in such a way that our minds are much more excited and active about pursuing a potential gain than they are eliminating a problem. Rewriting your statement into a positive objective channels and unleashes your mental powers. Now you're ready for the next step.

Step Four. Prioritize.

If you've done a good job daydreaming, you probably have a long list of things you'd like to accomplish. Unfortunately, you can't do everything. You just don't have enough time and energy to do *everything* you'd like to do. So, you must prioritize and select those things that are most important to you.

There's no formula for this, other than to think carefully about each of your daydreams, compare them to your situation, and select those that you feel are the most important to you. Remember to apply a dose of realism to this process. If you want to make $75,000 next year, for example, but you're currently in an $18,000 customer service position, that goal may not be very realistic.

Let's say you decide that your two most important goals for the year are to make a lot more money, and to save some money for your children's education.

Step Five. Specify.

This step requires you to turn your daydreams, which are often pretty vague at this point, into specific, achievable goals.

Let's take the first of the two examples, to make a lot more money. What's a lot more? After some reflection, you think along these lines: "I made $50,000 last year. If I can increase the business in my territory by 35 percent, I'll make $75,000. While that may seem like a lot, the economy has turned around and it is expanding. I have several new customers who are going to invest in major new equipment, and a few of my good customers are growing and expanding. If I work hard and smart, I may be able to do it."

Your earlier, vague goal of "making a lot more money," has now been turned into something very specific -- "making $75,000 in the new calendar year."

This is a key step in the process because the specific detail of the goal is part of what gives it power. If your goals are vague and abstract, they have less power to shape and direct your behavior.

You should now have a piece of paper with your specific, prioritized goals written on it. When you've reached that point, you're ready for the final step.

Step Six. Refine.

Because of the power of a goal to direct your behavior, it's very important that you write your goals

Chapter Fifteen: The Fifth Hat – Adept Human Resource Manager

exactly as you want them to be. A great deal of your time and effort will be directed toward achieving that goal over the next year. So, it behooves you to make sure the goal is right. You wouldn't want to waste some of that time and energy.

Once you have created written, specific goals, take a moment to judge them by some standards. See if they measure up to the following questions. If so, good. If not, rewrite them to meet the criteria listed below.

1. Are they specific?

Does each goal specify, in detail, exactly what you want to accomplish? Can you make it more specific than what it already is?

2. Are they measurable?

Can somebody else tell if you have achieved your goal? Have you stated it in measurable terms? Back to the example. To make a lot more money may be realistic, but it's not measurable. What's "a lot more?" By turning that phrase into a measurable unit, "$75,000," you have made your goal measurable.

3. Are they realistic?

Deciding to be elected president of the United States may be a worthwhile goal, but it may not be realistic for you. This is where your daydreams meet reality. Your goals should be a stretch and require you to work hard to accomplish them, but they shouldn't be so optimistic that you have no realistic chance of achieving them.

4. Do they have a specific time frame?

Every goal should have a deadline for completion. That helps put power into it. A goal with no deadline has little motivational power. For each goal, specify the date by which the goal will be attained.

In the example, the goal "To make $75,000 in the next calendar year," has a specific time frame. All the money has to be made by December 31st of that year.

5. Are they worthwhile?

Is this a valuable thing which, when it is attained, will be applauded by others? Is it something of which you'll be proud? You may have a very specific, measurable, realistic, time-sensitive goal such as this: *"to drink a case of beer four of every five evenings during the workweek, every week in the month of December."* While that goal meets all the other criteria, it's not very worthwhile. Your goals should be worthwhile.

This "refining" step is the last step of the goal-setting process. By the time you have finished it, you will have a written set of goals that express your view of your ideal accomplishments in a powerful, motivational way.

Applying the Goal-Setting Process to Improve Your Sales Results

It's easy to see that you can apply the goal-setting process in an unlimited number of ways. You can apply it to specific, day-to-day activities, like creating goals for every one of your accounts, for example. What do you want to accomplish this year, or this month, in each account? When you answer this question, you've set a goal.

On the other hand, you can apply the goal-setting process to more general, long-range issues, like your long-term financial, social, or spiritual progress.

In any case, it's the first step in gaining control of your time and becoming proactive. The only question is where to begin.

Think back to the onion analogy from chapter nine. Only this time, apply the concept of layers of depth in the onion to yourself. Illustration # 15-2 illustrates the application levels for goal setting. You can create goals for yourself at each level of the onion. On the most superficial level are goals having to do with your sales calls and your accounts. Goals at this level are necessary for you to take control of your sales time and become a proactive salesperson.

PERSONAL GROWTH FROM THE INSIDE OUT

Illustration 15-2

At the next level are goals for acquiring skills and sales techniques. This book, for example, should create a great number of those kinds of goals. The next level consists of goals having to do with your attitudes and personal growth. Finally, at the deepest level are goals having to do with your purpose in life and your reason for living. These are the deepest goals – spiritual issues – which effect every other goal above it.

Here's a list, starting from the surface and working downward, of the areas that I believe are worthy of your goal-setting efforts.
* Goals for every sales call.
* Goals for every "A" account.
* Annual sales, gross profit, and market share goals.
* Goals for the attainment of sales skills.
* Personal learning goals.
* Long-term goals for your career, finances, family social, spiritual and physical progress.
* An ultimate, "purpose in life" goal.

Where you start doesn't make much difference. I've found that you can begin at any level, and move upward or downward as you feel inclined. Sooner or later, however, you should address all the levels.

Review your long-term and annual goals once a year. I believe that you ought to take a day or so every year devoted to nothing but this process. Then, review your "A" account and short-term goals monthly, and write new ones for the coming months. Review your weekly and daily goals each week and each day, and create goals for your sales calls every day.

This goal-setting discipline will put you on the track to focused, directed behavior. And that is the first step of the salesperson who is becoming an effective human resource manager.

You're always more effective when you focus on unleashing your strengths, and managing your weaknesses. This was one of those principles that changed my life. As a younger man, much of my personal development efforts were focused on overcoming my weaknesses. I expended a lot of energy with little results.

Chapter Fifteen: The Fifth Hat – Adept Human Resource Manager

Then, as often happens to me, a comment someone made clicked in my brain, and I discovered the truth of this principle. I still recall the circumstances. It was a sermon by a minister in a Sunday morning worship service in a small church in Brighton, Michigan. I remember excitedly talking with him after the service. Of course! You'll always be more effective if you leverage your strengths, making the most of the talents and gifts you have, than trying to overcome your weaknesses.

You're probably familiar with the Pareto Principle. It's the 80/20 law. We often apply it to our customers. Eighty percent of our sales come from twenty percent of our customers. You'll find that to be close to true almost all of the time. In fact, you can apply the Pareto Principle to almost any area of human endeavor and find it to be true. So, it shouldn't be surprising to find that it's true about managing ourselves.

Eighty percent of our performance comes from twenty percent of our efforts. If we can discover the twenty percent that represents our strengths, and then learn to apply our energy to our strengths, we'll get far better results.

The trick is to discover your strengths, and then to develop ways in which they can be brought to bear on your current position. Here's an example from my life.

I discovered, early in my professional career, that I had a gift for speaking. I actually enjoyed speaking to groups of all sizes, and I was good at it. In fact, given a choice between making a one-on-one presentation, and talking to a group, I'd prefer the group.

Once I came to realize the truth of this principle, I tried to find ways to bring my "group presentation" skills to bear on my sales career. Whenever I was scheduled to make a presentation, I'd try to arrange for several of my customers to be there, rather than just one. I developed small seminars to train my customers in the use of my products, so that I could speak to them in groups, not just individually. I'd arrange for lunch meetings, where I brought lunches and made presentations to small groups. And I'd volunteer to speak at any gathering of my potential customers – trade shows, conferences, meetings, etc. These were all ways in which I could bring my strengths in speaking to my sales job. As a result, I multiplied my effectiveness and realized great success as a salesperson. It's no surprise then, that today, public speaking at conventions and national sales meetings is a major part of my practice.

Here's a process to use to implement this powerful principle.

Step One. Assess your strengths.
Who's the HR manager for you? You are! So, it's your responsibility to identify your unique set of strengths. Here are a couple of ways of doing it.
    1. Objectively think about yourself. Ask, and answer, these questions;
       a. What kinds of activities come very easy to you?
       b. What kinds of activities do you enjoy?
       c. What kinds of activities seem to get you the best results?

As you answer these questions, you'll often find a pattern developing. That pattern can be a good indication of where your unique strengths lie.
    2. Take a test. The science of assessment has come leaps and bounds in the last couple of decades. Some seemingly simple assessments can be almost frightening in how much they can tell you about yourself. Taking an

assessment or a battery of them can be one of the best things you do to reveal your own strengths and weaknesses.

Step Two. Get someone's validation/confirmation.

While it is up to you to identify your strengths, don't trust your own judgement completely. Once you have an idea of where your strengths lie, talk to someone who knows that part of you, and get their input. Your manager should be a great source of this validation, as should your spouse or significant other.

Listen carefully to their input, and revise your opinion accordingly.

Step Three. Find ways to apply those strengths to your job.

This is where your creativity can come into play. The more you are able to creatively apply your strengths to your job, the easier your job will become, and the more enjoyable it will be to you. There is no one formula for this part of the process because no combination of strengths and jobs is the same. So you have to figure this one out on your own.

I provided you the example of how I used my speaking ability in my sales positions. Now, it's up to you to apply your strengths to your situation.

Time Management

One of the most important areas to effectively manage is the use of your time. This is a larger issue for professional salespeople than for many other types of jobs because your time is so much in your control. You know that you could, if you chose to, spend hours a day not working, and it would be some time before your company realized it. What is far more likely than the salesperson who doesn't work, however, is the salesperson who spends hours not working *effectively*.

The difference is good time management. All this means that, if you're going to succeed in the Information Age economy, you must be more disciplined and smarter about using your time effectively than ever before.

Time management is a daily battle. You will never win the war. It's not like some big deal where, once it is done, you can look back and see a definite end to it. With time management, you rarely enjoy any kind of major feeling of accomplishment. Time management is not like that. There is no great victory.

Instead, there is a daily struggle. Some days you win more battles than others, but every day you're in the contest.

On one hand, you have all the forces that strive to suck away your energy and time. If you're not careful, you can spend most days being totally reactive. And, while there is some satisfaction in being incredibly busy taking care of other people's problems and concerns, in the end you have only worked everyone else's agenda while abandoning your own.

If you're going to be a successful Information Age salesperson, you need to work your own agenda. You need to take proactive control of your day and do the things that you know will be the best things to do. And that requires that every day you fight the battle for control of your time.

Ten Commandments for Good Sales Time Management

1. *Plan precisely for the use of your sales time.*

"Sales time" refers to the time when you're face-to-face with your customer. It's the fundamental reason for your job. Think about it. There is someone in your company who can do everything else that you do. But, the one thing you

Chapter Fifteen: The Fifth Hat – Adept Human Resource Manager

do that no one else does is meet with your customer face-to-face. It's the defining moment of your job. It's the part of your job through which you bring value to your company.

Unfortunately, it's very easy to go through the motions of each sales call without taking the time to plan. Most salespeople have only vague sales call plans, if any. From my own personal experience, as well my experience with the literally thousands of salespeople I've trained, I've come to the conclusion that it only takes three minutes to plan a sales call. So, a daily investment of about 15-20 minutes will provide you with almost all the planning time you will need to thoroughly plan for every sales call.

The results of sales calls that begin with a plan will be far greater than for those who have no plan. Without a plan, it's just too easy to get sidetracked and reactive. When you're finished with the day, you feel exhausted from all the problems you solved and the tasks you completed, but you haven't caused the things to happen that you wanted to make happen. So, you've spent your day busy, but ineffective. That's a luxury you can no longer afford.

Planning for the most effective use of your sales time will both increase the quantity, as well as improve the quality of face-to-face interaction with your customers.

You can apply an abbreviated version of the planning process from chapter three to the discipline of creating powerful sales call plans.

2. Plan to make good use of uncontrollable downtime.

You know what uncontrollable downtime is. It's those times that occur without notice, where your day was turned upside down through no fault of your own.

It's that moment when you've driven an hour to keep an appointment with someone you've been wanting to see, and he called in sick and nobody told you. All at once you're confronted with "uncontrollable downtime." The first temptation is to waste that time. I learned about uncontrollable downtime the hard way.

When I was selling surgical staplers, I often scrubbed with the surgeon who was learning to use the instruments. That's right. I was one of those people in caps, gloves and mask, standing over the patient, across from the surgeon, in the operating room. When they were just learning to use the instruments, surgeons liked to have me there in case they had any problems with the staplers. Most of the surgical procedures in which the staplers were used were major bowel and gastric surgery, and those cases were usually scheduled first thing in the morning, generally at 7:00 A.M.

I was working with a surgeon at a hospital about an hour's drive from my house. Since the case started at 7:00 A.M., I needed to get to the hospital at about 6:30 A.M. so that I could review the procedures and the instruments with the surgeon before scrubbing. That meant I had to leave my house around 5:00 A.M. But, since I always made it a practice to bring a box of donuts for the operating room nurses, I needed to leave at 4:30 A.M. to allow time to get to the donut shop. That meant getting up at 3:45 AM.

One of the common practices in a major surgery is to postpone a case if the patient has a fever. The surgical team never wants to add any stress to the patient if the patient has some kind of infection.

You guessed it. Three days in row, as I stumbled into the OR suite at 6:30 A.M., having already been awake for about three hours, the OR Supervisor glanced at the surgical schedule, looked up at me, and said, "Oh, didn't anyone call you? The case has been postponed!"

Chapter Fifteen: The Fifth Hat - Adept Human Resource Manager

On the third day, I decided the uncontrollable downtime was going to be an occupational hazard of my job and that, instead of becoming upset about it, I should take it in stride by being prepared for it.

Since then, I have always carried some work to do with me wherever I have gone. That way, I'm not frustrated by uncontrollable downtime.

You need to do the same. In your briefcase, always have some literature about that new product to study, or that quote you need to price, or that paperwork to be completed. By being prepared, you're always ready to make good use of uncontrollable downtime.

3. *Prioritize your activities every day.*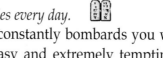

In a world that constantly bombards you with things to do, it's incredibly easy and extremely tempting to have your day shaped by the hundreds of demands and requests of everybody else.

I call this the "popcorn" approach to your workday. Imagine a popcorn popper, the old kind with a hot plate on the bottom and a glass canister above it. Visualize the popcorn kernels lying in the bottom of the hot plate, vibrating in the sizzling oil. When it gets hot enough, one of the kernels explodes and careens off the side of the canister and drops back into the oil. A few seconds later another explodes and bounces off a different portion of the canister. And then another shoots off in a third direction, another in yet another direction again and again. All that energy is dissipated as it shoots off in a countless number of directions.

That's an apt description of how some salespeople run their day. They are totally reactive to countless interruptions -- their energy exploding in a thousand different directions. The only real way to take control of all these temptations and interruptions is to create a priority list every day, and then stick to that list. That way you have a clear choice between working your agenda or working everyone else's.

If you have no priority list, then the choice is easy -- it's always everyone else's agenda that takes precedence. At the end of each day, before you go home and join your family, take about ten minutes and create a list of everything you want to do tomorrow. Then, go back and prioritize the items in order of importance. Which of all these items is the one which is likely to bring you the greatest result? After that, which is next? Number them in order of importance.

Then, tomorrow, when someone at the office wants you do something, realize that you have a choice. You can do what they want you to do, and that often means not doing what you want to do -- or you can work your agenda. Success belongs to the proactive salesperson, not the reactive one.

4. *Constantly evaluate the effectiveness of what you're doing.*

As a straight-commission salesperson, I created a couple habits that have served me well over the years. One was the habit of asking myself, several times during the course of the day, this question: "Am I doing, right now, that thing that is the most effective thing for me to do?"

I can't tell you how many hundreds or thousands of times my answer was "No." And, every time I answered myself in the negative, I then had to change what I was doing and do that thing which was the most effective. That habit has not only served me well as a straight-commission salesperson, but I find it to be one of my best time management tools as president of my own training and

Chapter Fifteen: The Fifth Hat – Adept Human Resource Manager

consulting business. My second habit was to *always do that which is hottest first*. In other words, if I had two or more things to do, I'd always do that thing that was "hottest" first. What's hottest? That's the second part of this habit. Hottest is *closest to the money*.

For example, if I had a choice between seeing one customer and closing the order, and seeing another to do a product demonstration, I'd close the order. That's closer to the money.

These two habits of daily time management can be powerful weapons you can use in your daily battle.

5. *Cluster similar activities.*

If you have ten phone calls to make, don't make two now, three later, and five this afternoon. Instead, make them all at one time. That way, the amount of time you spend transitioning to the next task will be significantly reduced.

6. *Create systems to handle routine tasks.*

We all have routine things that we must do over and over again. Fill out expense reports, create sales reports, complete other paperwork, file invoices, review back orders, etc.

You'll find that routine tasks can be handled very effectively if you create a system to handle them, and then always use that system to complete the task. You only have to think about the best way to do some of these routine tasks once.

For example, if you have to fill out a weekly expense report, always put your receipts in the same portion of your briefcase. Always fill out your form at the same time of the week, in the same place. Again, the duplication of routine efforts make them mindless things. And some things are best done mindlessly.

7. Use an appropriate strategy for the size and potential of the account.

Some accounts need more attention than others. It doesn't take a rocket scientist to figure that out. But developing that concept into a workable daily routine is something else. Review the discussion of ABC ratings in chapter three.

It means that some accounts should get a visit from you every six months and a phone call once a month. Others get two visits a week.

Don't be afraid to use a phone or fax to keep in contact with your low volume accounts. Invest your time in appropriate ways for the potential of each account you have. Do not treat everyone the same.

8. Don't go into the office!

It's my number one negative rule. It's based on Kahle's law of office time. Kahle's law is an inviolate observation about nature, that you can count on to the same extent that you count on the sun coming up every day. Kahle's law of office time says this. "If you plan on working in the office for 30 minutes, it will always take you two hours."

There is just something about going into the office that is inherently a time waster. People want to talk to you, you receive phone calls, there's mail to read, coffee to drink, and customer service people with whom to chat. Add that all up, and it's guaranteed to waste your time.

I once had one of my clients call me and ask about the design of a new office building she was erecting for her business. "What arrangements should I make for the salespeople?" she asked. "Should I build them each their own offices, or should I invest in those modular office systems so that each can have his own workspace?"

I replied, "You should have one phone in a very crowded place. Make it as difficult for them to work in the office as possible. That way they won't come there!"

That's how strongly I believe in this law. Whatever you do, stay out of the office!

But, if you must go in the office, and I recognize that sometimes you must, then go in the last thing in the day, not the first thing in the morning. If you go in at 4:30 in the afternoon with a half hour's worth of work to do, you're much more likely to get it done in 30 minutes than if you attempt the same thing at 8:00 in the morning.

9. *Be conscious of time wasters, and work to eliminate them.*

"Time wasters" are unconscious, time wasting habits you have created over the years. You've become so accustomed to them, that you're probably not even aware of them. So the first step is to become conscious of them.

For years I had an unconscious time waster. Every time I experienced a bad call -- something that didn't go the way I wanted it to, I had to find a coffee shop and buy myself a cup of coffee so that I could feel sorry for myself for 15 - 20 minutes. After that short pity party, I was ready to go back at it.

Then, one day, I realized what I was doing. Wasting all that time in a habit that didn't do me any good. I realized that self pity was a luxury I couldn't afford. So I worked to eliminate that habit of drinking coffee and feeling sorry for myself.

I suspect that you may have created some unconscious habits that fall into the category of time wasters. Here's a list I've gathered from my seminars as I've asked the participants to list some of their more cherished habitual time wasters. See if any of these sound familiar:

* Taking smoke breaks.
* Making personal calls.
* Running personal errands.
* Not making appointments -- just showing up unexpectedly.
* Small talk with people in the office.
* Not planning your day.
* Reading the morning paper.
* Taking long lunches.
* Eating lunch by yourself instead of with a customer.
* Taking long coffee breaks.
* Being unorganized.
* Trying to do everything yourself instead of relying on your support people.
* Not trusting the system, double-checking everything.
* Hand delivering paperwork to the office instead of mailing it in.

Got the idea? You may have a special little time waster that you've treasured for years. If you're going to be effective in our time-compressed age, now is the time to work to eliminate it.

10. Don't get caught up in immediate reaction.

Immediate reaction occurs when you have your day, or a portion of a day, planned, and then you receive a phone call or fax from one of your customers with a problem for you to solve. The natural tendency is to drop everything

Chapter Fifteen: The Fifth Hat – Adept Human Resource Manager

and work on the problem. After all, isn't that good customer service?

But, when you do that, you become reactive, and lose control of your day. So, isn't there some way to provide service but stay in control?

The problem is the assumption that just because someone calls, their problem is urgent and needs immediate attention. So, you immediately react. But that isn't necessarily true. Often, the situation isn't really urgent, and you can address it later.

All you need to do is ask this simple question of your customer. "Can I take care of it...(Fill in the most convenient time for you to do so.)" Sometimes, your customer will say, "Sure, that's OK." On those occasions, you will have regained control of your day again, and you can proceed with your plan.

Granted, sometimes it is an urgent issue. And on those occasions, you do need to take care of it as soon as you can. But, if you will ask the question, a good portion of the time you'll remain in control.

And, by asking the question, you refuse to get caught up in immediate reaction. Implement these ten commandments for good time management, and you'll make great strides in becoming an effective self-manager. You'll take your performance up a notch!

Chapter Sixteen:
Adept Human Resource Manager - Part II

In the previous chapter, we looked at the principles and processes you can use to direct your assets and energy into positive channels in order to leverage your strengths. No doubt, focusing on strengths and pursuing positive goals are powerful ways to unleash your potential.

Unfortunately, focusing on the positive is not the whole story. Even the most positive of people occasionally gets blindsided by adversity, hampered by depression, or frozen in fear. So, there is another side to this hat. Not only is it important to unleash your strengths, it's also important to overcome negative influences. These are the events and influences that knock you off course and dissipate your energies. Fear, depression, adversity, rejection – these are the negative forces that can side tract the most positive of salespeople. To be an effective human resource manager, you need to be adept at managing both positive as well as negative forces. Which brings us to the first of these principles: **You'll be more effective if you can eliminate the hindrances to your performance.**

Like so many of the principles, this one is also common sense applied to sales. The problem is not that salespeople don't agree with the validity of the principle, the problem is that they don't apply it.

Of course you'll be more effective if you can overcome the hindrances to your sales performance. We all have a memory of a call we didn't make because we were afraid of what we'd hear, or one that never happened because we told ourselves, "They won't buy, so why bother?" We all have had days when we've been too discouraged or depressed to give our best. And we've all had the experience of seeing some new technique or tactic, but never applying it because we were uncomfortable with it. All of these are examples of being hindered by negative forces. Let's look at some of the most common.

Handling Failure and Adversity

Failure is probably the professional salesperson's most common experience. You probably make less than 50 percent of the appointments you attempt to make. You probably sell less than 50 percent of the proposals or demonstrations you make. You fail more often than you succeed. If you don't have a way to handle this continuous failure, you'll find that it can affect you emotionally, hindering your performance, and maybe even driving you out of sales.

Dealing with failure is one of those skills that is rarely talked about, but absolutely essential to the success of a professional salesperson.

In my life, I certainly remember my failures more clearly than I do my successes. At one point in my sales career, I sold capital equipment. Specifically, amplification equipment for classrooms of hearing impaired children. These systems were sold to the special education school systems, and were big-ticket, budgeted items.

In one year, there were 29 deals available in my territory. Of those 29, I got 28 orders. But ask me which one

Chapter Sixteen: Adept Human resource Manager - Part II

I remember most clearly and which one I learned the most from. You know it -- my one failure.

Adversity is like failure in that it produces a negative situation for us. The difference is that adversity is not always our own doing. Failure is often a consequence of our own actions. It usually takes the form of the inability to achieve some objective or goal. So, when we fail, we don't achieve some positive thing for which we were striving. Adversity sometimes falls on us without any direct involvement of our part. It brings with it a negative situation – some pain that we weren't expecting. It hits all of us, not just professional salespeople. However, because salespeople live with failure and rejection so often, we are more susceptible to the negative consequences of adversity. It's easy to get depressed and down on ourselves when we fail if, at the same time, we're struggling with some kind of adversity.

One of my greatest challenges as a salesperson occurred in one of my sales positions. I had decided to leave the amplification equipment company, and accepted a position selling surgical staplers.

This was a major risk on my part. I was the number one salesperson in the nation for my current employer, had a good salary, a company car, and great prospects. However, I was bored and looking for another challenge. So I accepted a position which was the opposite in many ways. It paid straight commission, for example, with a draw that lasted only the first six months. The salespeople bought their own demonstration samples and literature from the company.

Before I accepted the offer, I calculated the amount of existing business in the territory. I felt that, if I could double the business within the first year, I'd be OK. After that, any increases would be real increases in my standard of living.

So I took the plunge and went off to New York for six weeks of intense training. While I was gone, the district sales managers changed, and I had a new boss. When I returned home from training, I was quickly met by my new district sales manager, who announced that he had rearranged the territories. And surprise, the territory for which I was hired wasn't exactly the territory I was actually going to receive. In fact, the territory I ended up with had only about 30 percent of the existing business on which I was depending. My livelihood and the health and well being of my family was in serious jeopardy.

I was outraged. How could they do this to me? What kind of a company was this that would treat its employees that way? I immediately decided that I didn't want to work for them and began looking for a different job. However, it only took a few weeks of interviewing for me to realize that I was seen as unemployable. Most people with whom I interviewed viewed my quick desire to leave as a weakness in me, not my company.

One thing led to another and, after six months, I owed the company $10,000 (a lot of money in the mid-70's), my draw was finished, and I had few prospects for finding another job. Talk about being between a rock and a hard place!

That was adversity, compounded by my failure to effectively sell the product. How do you deal with failure and adversity? Here's a process that will work for you.

Step One. Accept the new reality.

No use moping about it. No use pretending that it'll go away or change or that it doesn't matter. It *does* matter or else you wouldn't be thinking about it. Accept that you failed. Accept that your situation is not what you'd like it to be. Once you accept it, and stop denying it or fighting it, you can go on from there.

At the same time that you accept the new reality, accept your responsibility to do something about it. No one is going to bail you out. The reality is that you're in this situation, and *you* need to do something about it.

When I was in the middle of my struggle with my failure under the new manager, I finally saw, in a moment of blinding clarity, that my situation was pretty much my own doing. It wasn't them, it was *me*! The realization of my personal responsibility was like a great weight off my shoulders. If the problem was me, I could do something about it! I was once again in a situation where I could influence the world around me and affect my life. I was no longer a victim, depressed under the unjust weight of someone else's actions.

And, since the problem was me, the power to do something was also in me!

Step Two. Ask questions.

This is a great time to learn. Remember, you'll generally learn more from your failures than you will from your successes, providing that you're ready and able to learn. One effective way to learn is to reflect on what happened and ask questions about it. How did it happen? Why? What did you do (not do) to bring this situation about? What could you have done differently? How did your customer react? How did your competitor act? Is there some lesson in that? Got the idea? Begin with questions.

In my situation, my question-asking routine led me to the conclusion that my own bitterness and negativity was the major problem. If I could do away with that, I could be more effective.

Step Three. Draw conclusions.

Once you ask the questions, answer them fully. After each question you ask about the situation, follow it with this question that you ask about yourself: "What should I do differently in the future?"

If you ask, "What did I do to create this situation?" and your answer is, "I didn't thoroughly prepare my presentation," then ask the second question, "What should I do differently in the future?" The answer to that question is your conclusion: "I should make sure I am thoroughly prepared for every presentation."

These conclusions, or reflections on your behavior, are the single most important fruits of your failure. ==Almost any failure is worthwhile if it stimulates some changed behavior and deeper understanding on your part==. It's not what happens that's important in the long run -- it's what you learn from it that counts.

I began drafting this book in the Spring of 1998, when my Detroit Red Wings had won their second Stanley Cup Championship. Two sweeps of opponents two years in a row. It was truly an exciting moment, made even more delectable by talks of the beginning of a winning dynasty. Shortly after the final game Darren McCarty, one of Red Wings, reflecting on the team's previous years of failure, remarked, "You have to lose before you can win." He meant, of course, that losing (or failure), if you learn from it, is a necessary stepping stone to success.

That's a powerful principle that's worth spotlighting: **If you learn from it, failure is an incredibly powerful step towards success.**

In my situation, I concluded that I needed to stimulate myself to be positive and to overcome my bitterness and resentment with positive self-confidence.

Step Four. Play with situations.

Start little what-if games in your imagination. If you're in a miserable situation, begin by asking yourself questions like, "What if I did this....?" or "What if I did that...?"

See if this doesn't stimulate some creative, and exciting possibilities for you. I asked myself how I could overcome my internal bitterness and resentment. I did the "what-if" games and came up with a novel approach. I decided that I needed to change my attitudes. I was caught in a negative mode, and I needed to change that to a positive mode. I reasoned that I needed to put positive, confident thoughts into my head. If I could fill my head with positive thoughts, I'd gradually be able to change my negative attitude.

At the time, I was living on the outskirts of my territory, and I had a daily 45-minute drive into the metropolitan Detroit area on Interstate 96. I decided to make use of that 45 minutes every morning to put positive thoughts into my head.

I spent an evening finding all the powerful, positive promises in the Bible, and wrote them on 3" X 5" cards. Then, each morning, I'd hold the 3" X 5" cards in front of me on the steering wheel, and flip through them over and over -- reading them repetitively as I drove into the city. As I bathed my mind in positive, confident ideas, I slowly changed my attitude, and began to turn my bitterness and resentment into optimism.

Step Five. Focus on short-term possibilities.

When life seems to have dealt you the most unfair blow, and the future looks miserable, stop contemplating the future. It's no fun thinking about how miserable you're going to be. Instead, focus on the short-term possibilities.

I'm a great believer in long-term goals. But I also have been through enough miserable situations in my life to know that there are times when it's best to forget (for now) those long-term goals and focus on the positive things you can do *today*!

I can not tell you how many times in my life I've found this discipline to be a powerful tonic to a depressed view of the future. Instead of thinking about next year, think about tomorrow. What positive things can you do tomorrow? Or, better yet, today. What's the single most positive thing you can do today? Give yourself realistic, short terms goals. And, I mean really short term -- today and tomorrow. Think in terms of positive actions. You may not be able to create any long-term or mid-term goals in your current state of mind, but you still have the ability to select right from wrong, good from bad, and positive from negative. So, focus on the very short term. Do the most positive things you can think of to do today, and don't worry about long-term goals.

Back to my situation. With no draw, no commissions, no salary, and lots of financial responsibilities, I couldn't think in terms of my long-term financial goals. I decided to focus on today and tomorrow, and do the best things I could do short term. Instead of thinking about developing some account next month, I'd visit it today. I discovered a discipline I turned into a habit which was to serve me well from then on. Several times during the course of the day, I'd ask myself, "Am I doing the thing that is the single most

Chapter Sixteen: Adept Human resource Manager - Part II

effective thing for me to be doing right now?" If the answer was "no," I would change what I was doing.

At the same time, I remember deciding that, outside of my working day, the single most positive thing I could do was exercise. It always made me feel better. I knew it to be a good thing. So I began an exercise program.

Were these two things strategically designed to meet some long-term goal of mine? No! Were they my best response for the need to do something positive every day? You bet!

In neither case was I focused on long-term goals. However, I wasn't in the kind of circumstance where I felt long-term goals were possible. I couldn't see how I was going to survive my current mess. So, I focused on the very short-term positive things I could do today.

When I was squarely in the middle of the rock and hard place trying to sell surgical staplers, I couldn't imagine paying off that $10,000 debt. So I didn't think about it. Instead, I focused on using each day in the most positive way I could.

Step Six. Act.

Sooner or later, you've got to do something. There is something about action that begets more action. If you can't figure out what to do, and you're caught in a confused mental or emotional paralysis, force yourself to *do something*. It really doesn't matter what you do, as long as you start doing. Once you get moving, you'll find it easier to move in positive and thoughtful ways.

I've found that when I'm in the middle of a funk brought on by miserable circumstances or my own failure, I become paralyzed by my own thoughts. One of the most helpful things to do is to do something. Act! Stop thinking and do something! Action begets action. Start moving and you'll quickly feel like moving some more.

And, oh yes, in case you're wondering -- in six months I was able to pay off the debt, and I began making more money than I had imagined possible. What was an absolutely hopeless and miserable situation changed into one of the most financially rewarding, satisfying experiences of my life.

Surviving the Tidal Wave of Information

There is a new threat to salespeople bearing down on you. Here's the issue: Because of the rapid explosion in the quantity of information sloshing around us, it's easy to be overwhelmed and rendered ineffective by the sheer amount of it. Think of how many product brochures you need to review every year, how many memos from the higher-ups, how many reports of various types, pricing information, service bulletins – and that's just on the internal side of the business. Then factor in the amount of information being generated by your customers – their needs and interests, the names and situations of each of their key contacts, their changing product lines, concerns and competitors. Now stir in the process information, the tools and procedures you use to do your job. That's the new computer program, forms, phone numbers, fax sheets, form letters, email and internet information. Finally, pour in the marginal information that can be enticing yet not very productive. That's the 102 TV stations we can now get on our digital cable, the slew of unsolicited email messages, the growing pile of bulk mail enticements, the 40,000+ new books published in the US alone each year, and the new publications and newsletters in whatever format.

All these pieces of the information tidal wave are hardly droplets by themselves. But when added together and dumped at you in the typical week, they can be a tidal wave of information, washing you away under their sheer quantity, and rendering you ineffective. When I've taught my module on information management to salespeople at my seminars, I've often asked them how many could spend at least eight hours a week doing nothing but considering all the information that comes their way each week. The resulting show of hands is often unanimous. Think of it, at least eight hours a week doing nothing but dealing with the tidal wave of information. That's 20% of the work week. And that's minimal. Which brings us to our next principle: **The quantity of information which comes your way can render you ineffective.**

If you're going to become a skillful practitioner of the fifth hat, then you need to be adept at information management. In chapter three we discussed the issue of information management from the perspective of collecting and using good information in order to enable you to make good decisions, and create effective plans. In this chapter, we're discussing information management from the perspective of gaining control of the amount of information so that you will not be rendered ineffective.

Information Management Process

Step One. Develop some criteria for screening most of the information that comes to you.

Look at illustration # 16 - 1.

MANAGING INFORMATION

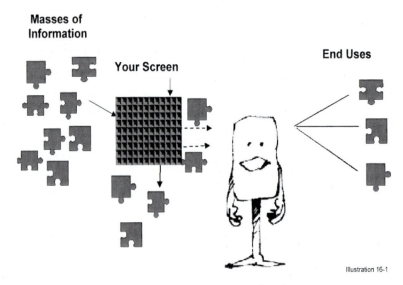

Illustration 16-1

Because of the great quantity of information coming at you, you need a device to filter some of it out so that you never spend more than a few seconds looking at it. It's like a screen window on your house. It lets some things through, but also keeps a lot of undesirable things out. When it comes to information, you have a similar situation. You want to protect yourself with a screen around you that allows some information through but also keeps a lot of undesirable details out. There are a number of possibilities. You can use software to screen out some email messages, voice mail to screen out phone calls, a good secretary or assistant to screen out people wanting to see you, etc. You'll have to develop your own screen based on your situation.

At some point, however, you'll need to personally apply a screen to the incoming information. That screen should be the concept of "USEFUL.' In other words, every piece of information that comes at you ought to first be pressed through the filter of the question, "Is this likely to be useful to me?" If the answer is "No, it may be interesting, it may be entertaining, but it probably won't be useful," then don't spend any more time with it. Get rid of it immediately. If the answer is "Yes, this is likely to be useful," then consider it further.

So, let's say you've arrived at the office, and emptied your mailbox. There's a memo from the boss regarding a sales meeting coming up. That's useful. There's a new report showing the number of units you sold of some product this year versus the number sold last year. You use the screen of "useful," decide that it's not likely to make any difference to you, and toss it. There's a series of price increases for products you rarely sell. You decide the time it takes to study and file those isn't worth it, and toss those. There's an article written by one of your customers that was published in a trade journal. Your boss has made a photo copy for you. You decide this might be useful to read. There are four messages that people have called. Two are from customers, so you set those aside to answer. The third is from a credit card company, with a new credit card to offer you. You toss that. The fourth is from one of the other salespeople in your company. You decide to return that call. And so on.

Applying the screening question, "Is this likely to be useful?" to every piece of information and demand for your time allows you to eliminate much of it right away, and thus protect a portion of your time from the tidal wave of information that presses on you daily.

Step Two. Determine the end uses of the information you consider.

Now, consider the information that's left. If it's useful, it has a use. So, where are you going to use it? Let's think of all the possibilities. You'll certainly want information about your customers, so why not develop a set of customer files? One manila folder for each A and B customer, and perhaps one for all of your C customers. Then, perhaps, an electronic duplicate of that file system in which to keep electronic information.

You'll also want information about your competitors. So, develop an electronic and hard copy file for each of your major competitors.

You'll want information about the products and services you represent. So, a set of files for each of those is appropriate.

Then you'll want information about the processes you use to bring together your products with your customers. Those files would include information about how to use the computer system, the reports and forms your company uses, etc.

As a subset of those, you'll want files for good ideas about your own personal development – those behaviors and skills that you want to improve or add to your repertoire.

Now, when you look at the pile of stuff in your mailbox, or all those email messages on your screen, you'll look at them with a new perspective. Consider each piece that has made it through the initial screening. Where or how will you use it? File it in the appropriate place.

But what if something doesn't fit into one of these prearranged files? You've got to question your initial judgement. If you can't think of where it would be useful, perhaps it isn't useful, and it should be discarded.

Once you have your information appropriately arranged according to its end use, you're ready for step three.

Step Three. Handle the information.

In other words, use it. Remember, if it's useful, you should be able to use it. So, what are you doing to do with it? That memo from the boss, for example. You read the memo, make some notes in your daytimer or computer, and then toss the memo. You acted on it. You used it.

That article written by one of your customers first went into that customer's folder. Then, as you prepare for your next sales call, you review the article, and decide to complement the customer on it. You may even highlight a couple things to talk to him about. So, you file that with the materials for your next sales call, and prepare to use it then.

You'll find that some information is worth studying, some should be filed and acted on at a later date, and some should be acted on immediately.

Discipline yourself to implement this process, and you'll find yourself staying afloat in the tidal wave of information.

Dealing With Fear

One of the biggest obstacles to the success of any salesperson, yourself included, is fear. Fear reveals itself in a number of ways -- any one of which can sap your energy and diminish your success. First is the fear of rejection, often said to be a salesperson's single biggest obstacle. It's the fear of rejection that keeps you from calling on new accounts or meeting new people within your current accounts. We are all -- at some level -- afraid that we'll get turned down, and we don't like that feeling.

I recall my first professional sales call. I had to demonstrate a speech therapy instrument to a PhD speech pathologist. I had never demonstrated anything to anyone before. I was so scared and nervous that my hands were shaking. On top of everything, my district manager was with me, observing my performance! After the call, he asked me if I was aware that I was clenching and unclenching my fist over and over. Evidently, I was so tense that I was not conscious of my actions. That's fear.

Second is the fear of stretching yourself into areas beyond your comfort zone. This may be the experienced, professional salesperson's most common fear. You have worked hard to create a large group of people who know you, generally like you, and are willing to spend time with you -- they are your customers. And you have a set of products or services with which you've grown very comfortable. More importantly, you have created a number of habits - ways in which you go about your job - which generally have been successful for you.

Since it's taken you some time to get to this point, you're naturally hesitant to do anything to jeopardize the status quo. That means that it's difficult to push beyond the comfortable discussions you're accustomed to having. You're a little afraid to try some of the principles and processes I have discussed in earlier sections of this book.

And this fear keeps you in a rut -- stuck in the performance levels to which you've become accustomed. Stuck in the behavior patterns that have become comfortable for you.

With most salespeople, it's not the fear of big things that is the issue, it's the fear of a thousand small things -- all related to jeopardizing your fragile hold on your customers and your status quo.

It may be that none of these issues affects you. In that case, great -- move on to the next section. But, if you've ever been afraid to try something new in your job, afraid to be held accountable for some level of performance, afraid to stretch outside of your comfort zones, then you need to know how to deal with that fear.

Here's a process to help you overcome fear and successfully stretch yourself to new levels of productive behavior.

Step One. Identify the issue.

The first step in overcoming fear is to recognize that it is fear that is hindering you. I can remember more than a few miserable hours I weathered sitting at a desk trying to work up the courage to make cold calls. What stopped me was my fear of rejection. And it took several hours of mental games before I realized that fear was the issue. I was afraid.

And, until I realized that fear was the problem, I was powerless to overcome it. When you find yourself hesitant to do something -- particularly if that thing is something new -- ask yourself if the real issue isn't that you're afraid.

If you find yourself hesitant to meet new people, present a new product line, or try a new selling tactic, look inward and see where that hesitancy is coming from. If it's fear, acknowledge it, and move forward.

Step Two. Look for deeper causes.

Once you've decided that fear is the problem, think about *why* you may be afraid. Have you had a bad experience in the past? Is this something like a similar experience? Then, argue with yourself. For example, if you discover you're afraid because of a bad past experience, argue with yourself. Tell yourself that was only one experience, and now you're older and wiser.

This process of arguing with yourself can provide logical support for you to attack your own fear. You can literally talk yourself out of your fear by reasoning with yourself.

Step Three. Remind yourself of past successes.

If arguing with yourself doesn't work, remind yourself of a past success you've achieved by doing the thing that you now fear. I finally overcame my fear of cold calling by putting a picture of one of my best customers -- a customer I had acquired initially via a cold call -- next to the phone. When I felt hesitant to make those cold calls, I'd pull the picture out, and remind myself of my past success in dealing with that fear.

Step Four. Remind yourself of future rewards.

What will happen if you are successful at doing this thing you fear? Will you earn more money? Acquire new customers? Provide yourself with a strategic advantage? If so, remind yourself of that thing that you want. You may even put an illustration or picture of it by the phone or in your car where you can be reminded of your goal.

Often, that visual reminder of your future rewards will be enough to stimulate you to action.

Step Five. Remind yourself of past rewards.

Have you been successful in the past? Have you enjoyed the rewards of that success? Then remind yourself of some of your past rewards when you find yourself hesitant to do something.

Chapter Sixteen: Adept Human resource Manager - Part II

Step Six. ACT! ACT! ACT!

Regardless of which of these techniques work for you, the important thing to do is *act*. Sooner or later, you must do something. Until you turn your thoughts into action, you haven't been successful. Ultimately, the only way to overcome fear is to act. All the other things that I've talked about are only a means to an end. They are self-management tools you can use to bring yourself to the point where you can act. *Action* is the final victory over fear.

Dealing With Adversity: Learned Optimism

In 1992, Dr. Martin Seligman published a book that may become one of the most significant books of the decade. In it, he describes his lifework. As a research psychologist, Dr. Seligman began by studying helplessness in dogs. In an early experiment, he put dogs into a cage from which they could not escape, and subjected them to mild shocks. After some effort at escape, the dogs would give up trying and lay down. Later, he put them into a cage from which they could easily escape, and subjected them to the same mild shocks. The dogs would just lay down and give up. Surprisingly, they did not attempt to remove themselves from the irritant. They had learned helplessness and hopelessness.

In subsequent experiments, Dr. Seligman found a similar behavior in human beings. Put into a room and subjected to irritating noises from which they could not escape, they soon learned to give up. When put into a room with a mechanism that would turn off the noise, they still didn't try. They had learned helplessness and hopelessness.

From this beginning, Dr. Seligman continued to formulate a thesis he calls "learned optimism." It says, basically, that human beings learn to have either a pessimistic or an optimistic outlook. Dr. Seligman's book contains a self-assessment to measure the degree of pessimism or optimism of the reader.

Dr. Seligman's thesis arises from the way people explain negative events to themselves. When something negative happens, as it eventually will, the way you explain it to yourself determines your pessimistic/optimistic attitude. There are three components of this "explanatory style."

The first component is the degree to which you believe the event to will be *permanent*. Pessimists believe negative events will be permanent, while optimists believe that they will be temporary.

The second component is *pervasiveness*. Pessimists believe the causes of negative events are universal, affecting everything they do. Optimists believe them to be specific, and limited to the individual circumstances.

The third component is *personal*. Pessimists believe that negative events are caused by themselves. Optimists believe that the world is at fault.

Here's how this behavioral perspective works in the everyday life of a salesperson.

Let's say you visit one of your large accounts, and your main contact announces that the vice-president for operations has signed a prime vendor agreement with your largest competitor, and that all of your business will be moved to that competitor within the next 30 days. *That's* a negative event.

As you drive away from the account, you think to yourself, "I blew it here. I should have seen it coming. I'm never going to learn this job. I'll blow the next one too. I mismanage them all."

Chapter Sixteen: Adept Human resource Manager - Part II

Now, that's a pessimistic explanation of the event. Notice that you have explained it in a way that is personal, "*I* blew it." Your explanation is also permanent, "I'm *never* going to learn to do this job," and pervasive, "I mismanage them *all*."

Now stop a minute, and analyze how you feel as a result of this explanation. Probably defeated, dejected, depressed, and passive. These are not the kinds of feelings you need to energize you to make your next sales call.

Let's revisit the situation, this time offering optimistic explanations. The same event occurs -- you receive bad news from your best account. As you drive away, you think to yourself, "They really made a bad mistake this time. It's a good thing the contract is only for a year. That gives me time to work to get it back. I'm glad it was only this account and no others."

That's an optimistic explanation because your explanations were not personal, permanent, or pervasive. How do you feel about your future as a result of this explanation? Probably energized and hopeful.

See the difference? The event was the same. The only difference was the way you explained it to yourself. One set of explanations was optimistic, leading to energy and hope, while the other was pessimistic, leading to dejection and passivity.

Dr. Seligman has isolated optimistic behavior as one of the characteristics of successful people. Using various techniques he's developed, he predicted elections by analyzing each candidate's explanatory style. The most optimistic candidates often win elections.

The implications for you are awesome. If you can improve your explanatory style, and make it more optimistic, you'll create more positive energy and hope for yourself, no matter how difficult or negative the circumstances with which you must deal.

Learned optimism can be one of your most powerful self-management techniques. It's based on this powerful principle: **Your thoughts influence your feelings and your actions, and you can choose your thoughts**.

Here's the process Dr. Seligman recommends.

Step One. Analyze your explanatory habits.

Wait until you must deal with some negative event or some adversity in your life. Then, stop and observe what you are telling yourself about the event. What do you believe about yourself and the reason why bad things happen? In chapter nineteen we'll be discussing this issue of 'world-view' and your personal mission. That discussion will help put this in perspective. For now, ask to what degree your explanations are personal, permanent or pervasive?

Step Two. Note the consequences of your explanatory style.

Pessimistic explanations always lead to passivity and dejection. Optimistic explanations always lead to energy and hope. Which is more likely to propel you to future success?

Step Three. If you're pessimistic, you must change the way you think.

Your future success, your ability to achieve all your goals depends on your ability to rise up and meet adversity with renewed energy and optimism. You can do this by choosing to think differently.

Dr. Seligman makes the following suggestions.

Distract your thoughts. In other words, when you find yourself thinking negative and pessimistic thoughts, tell yourself to "Stop!" You can even say it out loud, or shout it to yourself. Just "STOP" thinking those things.

Then, shift your thoughts to something else. I'd suggest you think about something that brings you pleasure or satisfaction, or something at which you're good.

Dispute your explanations. This is a longer-lasting approach. Argue with yourself. Reason your way out of your negative thoughts. Look at the evidence, or suggest alternatives. Reason from the implications or usefulness of what you're thinking.

Back to our example. On the way out to your car after your miserable call, you are thinking to yourself "I blew it here. I should have seen it coming. I'm never going to learn this job. I'll blow the next one, too. I mismanage them all."

When you catch yourself thinking defeating thoughts, argue with yourself. Think, "Wait a minute, while it's true I may have been able to do something if I had seen this coming, the truth is that the VP would never see me. The other company must have had some special in. That doesn't mean that this will work anywhere else. It's just this account. There certainly isn't any evidence of this possibility happening anywhere else. And, the truth is that the entire purchasing department is not happy about this course of events. If I stay close to the account, they may find lots of reasons to continue to do business with me."

What you've done is argue with yourself in order to change your thought processes. As a result of thinking differently, you have more energy, more hope and, therefore, more likelihood of success in the future.

You can change your thoughts. You can choose to think differently. You can choose to believe differently.

And that fundamental decision about how you think can, more than any other single decision, affect your future success.

Dr. Seligman has discovered, through his scientific research, a truth that has been known for thousands of years. The Apostle Paul, writing in the book of Romans, counseled new Christians to, "Be transformed by the renewing of your mind." And Solomon said that, "As a man thinks in his heart, so is he."

Your choice of what to think about, and how to think about what happens to you, is one of the most important choices you'll ever make.

If you're going to become a master of the fifth hat, choose your thoughts wisely.

Trying on This Hat

I know, you're overwhelmed. I would be, too. This hat, Adept Human Resource Manager, contains more principles and processes than any other. And no wonder. You're an incredibly complex, potentially powerful entity. Managing yourself in order to wring the most value from your strengths and abilities is a complex, never-ending challenge. Let's start by reviewing the principles:

1. You're always more effective when you set goals.
2. You're always more effective when you focus on unleashing your strengths and managing your weaknesses.
3. You'll be more effective if you can eliminate the hindrances to your performance.
4. If you learn from them, failure and adversity can be incredibly powerful steps toward success.
5. The quantity of information which comes your way can render you ineffective.

Chapter Sixteen: Adept Human resource Manager - Part II

6. Your thoughts effect your feelings and your actions, and you can control your thoughts.

That's a lot to incorporate into your life. But you do have some very effective processes to assist you with the task. They include processes designed for:
* goal-setting
* unleashing strengths
* dealing with fear
* handling failure & adversity
* information management
* learned optimism

So how do you work all this into your life?

Reflecting on my experience, I'd suggest you start with identifying your strengths. I recall that insight being such a powerful turning point in my life, that I expect it may well have the same impact on you. So, begin there, and build some energy and momentum from the realizations and successes that process generates in your life.

You can't really decide to implement the processes for handling adversity and failure until you find yourself in those situations. Don't be impatient. You'll be suffering from one or the other soon enough. Keep this book as a reference, remembering that there is some insight to help you when those negative forces descend on you.

Until then, keep the focus positive. Set goals. Go all the way back to the first hat, Astute Planner, and find the suggestions in the "Trying on the first hat" section. Each of those planning sessions are first opportunities to set goals.

When you have uncovered your strengths and set goals, you'll find yourself moving along in a powerful and positive pattern. Add the other processes as you have time and occasion.

And that will get you a good start to implementing the fifth hat.

 Wearing the Hat

Confident. Self-assured. Those are powerful characteristics. That's how you'll feel when you begin to gain the competencies that compose the fifth hat. You'll have the knowledge that you're working in the most effective ways you can, that you're using the strengths and gifts your creator put into you, that you know how to survive the difficult days of a salesperson's life.

But most of all, you'll have the knowledge, the assurance that comes from experience, that you're gaining mastery of the greatest obstacle a salesperson has – himself! This will really take your performance up a notch!

Chapter Seventeen:
Using the Six Hats to Take Your Performance Up-A-Notch

Challenge: I have so much paperwork and other things to do, that I don't have enough time to sell.

This is another one of those issues that can render you ineffective and sidetrack your career. Generally speaking, your company pays you to bring money into the organization, either by creating new customers, or expanding the business with current customers. If you spend your time doing other things, you're jeopardizing the value you bring to your company.

It may be that your job description includes other duties in addition to selling. In my experience, that situation almost always leads to less and less time spent selling, and more time spent doing the operational side of your job. That's because it's always much easier to react to the operational tasks that present themselves than it is to proactively create activity on the sales side. The "other stuff" invariably expands and pushes the sales efforts out of your day. It's so common, in fact, that I have an acronym for it: the *dreaded OSE (other stuff expansion)*. If you're in a hybrid job, part sales and part operations, you are particularly susceptible to OSE.

Even if you are not in a hybrid position, you are purely a salesperson, you are still vulnerable to OSE. There are reports to read, memos to peruse, new sell sheets to study, invoices to file, notes to rewrite, inside people to converse with, other salespeople to ruminate with, the list of OS goes on and on. With the incredible expansion of information that marks the Information Age, you're vulnerable to being rendered ineffective by the sheer mass *of stuff.*

 Applying the Six Hats

This is an example of the kind of real life problems that seriously impact the day to day life of a salesperson. It's not the kind of thing you are taught in a sales training class, but it does significantly impact your performance and your career.

To handle this challenge, you really only have three options. First, you can do nothing, and continue to work your job in the same way that you have been. As long as you're meeting your goals and your company is happy with your performance, there's no reason to change.

But, for most salespeople, one of the two parties mentioned above – you or your company - is becoming unhappy. Some change must happen or you'll find yourself in a situation you don't want to be in.

So, either your company changes its expectations of you, or you change the way you're doing your job. Let's work on the first issue.

Put on your fourth hat (Skillful Influencer), only this time the focus of your skills is not your customers, it's your company. Treat your company like a customer. Identify the power structures and political connections inside your organization. Spend some time with your manager and other the key people trying to understand their SPOO and PIE as it relates to your job description. Then, carefully prepare your case for a redefinition of your job just like you'd prepare a major presentation to a customer. Make that presentation using the principles and processes outlined in the chapters on the fourth hat. Hopefully, this effort will be successful and you'll have been able to influence your company to change.

Unfortunately, it doesn't always work that way. Your company, for a variety of reasons, decides not to change. In which case *you* are the party who must change. This is the place to exercise the discipline to stick to some of the processes outlined in chapter fifteen on time management. This is an effective spot to exercise your skills as an HR manager, making sure that you're managing yourself to wring out the most effective application of your greatest asset – yourself.

Begin by staying out of the office as much as possible. If you must go into the office, go at the very latest point that you can in the course of the day. In other words, don't go in the first thing in the morning, rather, go in the last thing in the day. That will free up some of your selling time. Remember the rule of OSE (other stuff expansion). If you go into the office the first thing in the morning, you'll suffer OSE and not get out to the selling side of your job until way past when you thought you'd be at it.

Use your goal-setting process to set specific goals for the selling side of your job, and spend a lot of time in planning and preparing for each day. If you don't proactively attack that portion of the day devoted to selling, the reactive portion devoted to other stuff will invariably creep in to push out selling time. So, you'll need to be even more disciplined about planning and preparing.

Cultivate relationships with the support staff in your company, and try to download as much of your non-selling stuff to them as possible. They can return some calls, check on the status of orders, mail out samples and literature, and solve customer problems. The list of potential things your company's support staff could do for you is limited only by your imagination.

In all of this, your disciplined application of principles and processes from the fifth hat will be crucial. The key word here is disciplined. That means that ==every day you're going to have to fight the battle for the effective use of your time.== Discipline yourself to practice these processes daily. Should you put down your discipline and relax, OSE will roar back with a vengeance and render that day ineffective.

You know what to do, and you know how to do it. The key to long-term victory over OSE is your disciplined implementation.

Chapter Eighteen:
The Sixth Hat - Master Learner

The sixth hat is my favorite. It's the fundamental, foundational hat. The competencies related to it provide the support for all the other hats. Without mastering this hat, you'll find it very difficult to master the others.

Picture a tree (illustration #18 – 1).

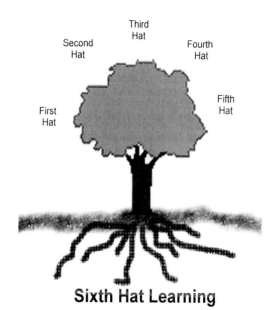

Illustration 18-1

The roots are hidden beneath the surface. The trunk, branches and leaves are the parts we see. Yet, the roots are what bring support and sustenance to all the other parts.

So it is with the sixth hat. These are the competencies that lie beneath the surface, that support and sustain all the others. With the sixth hat, the other, more visible, hats will constantly grow and thrive, providing you a lifetime of personal and career success. Without it, you'll eventually wither under the onslaught of the turbulent environment.

Remember the discussion of turbulent times in chapter one? Let's revisit that for a moment. We observed that we live in times that are changing at a more rapid pace than at any time in the history of the human race.

In light of that, it's my belief that the only sustainable, effective response to a rapidly changing world is cultivating the ability to change ourselves. The first five hats provide direction, structure and focus in your quest to change yourself. Together, they describe a powerful and effective approach to the changing situations that you and other salespeople face. When the need is to change and grow, they show you the branches and twigs on which that growth should take place.

But the task before you can be overwhelming. To this point, we've discussed dozens of principles and processes. You can't possibly implement all of them instantly. So how do you sort it out? How do you prioritize, focus and begin the process of implementing the hats? How do you gain those competencies that I've discussed? And how do you do it in a way that reflects the speed demanded by our changing world? How do you master a hat in a few months, rather than a few years?

It's one thing to understand the concepts, principles and processes of the Six Hats, but it's another to actually act on them. The underlying question is, "How do you make the Six Hats a part of your daily routine?" The answer? – you've got to learn.

Chapter Eighteen: The Sixth Hat – Master Learner

I know that sounds trite, but it isn't. Learning, no -- learning to learn – is the greatest of all the hats. It's the root system for all the growth that takes place above it. If you're going to become a master of the Six Hats, you must change your behavior so that you are acting with knowledge of the Six Hat principles and implementing the Six Hat processes.

So, the underlying issue – the core problem for you – is to quickly and effectively learn. That word might be giving you some problems. When we hear the word "learning" it often brings back images of our days in high school or college, sitting in classes and absorbing somewhat irrelevant information. That's one definition of learning, but it's not what I'm talking about. In the Information Age, the only real useful learning is that which results in changed behavior.

In other words, if you think you've learned something but you haven't changed the way you act, you haven't really learned. Learning is synonymous with changed behavior.

Here's my definition. Think of it as the primary principle behind the first hat: **Learning is the process of taking in new information, or developing new insights, and then changing your behavior in positive ways as a result.**

"Continuous personal growth," "continuous improvement," and "rapid development" are all other, equally accurate terms. The problem for many of us is that we never really learned how to learn. Sure we learned how to earn grades in school, but I'm talking about real life here, not academics. Academics is primarily concerned with what goes on in your head. I, on the other hand, am primarily concerned with how you act. We all know there is often no real connection between academic learning and real life effectiveness. I'm sure every reader of this book knows someone who was a good student, academically, but something less than successful in real life.

I'm sure some of you are thinking, "But I can learn. Look, I've gotten this far. Isn't that an indication of my ability to learn?"

Sure it is. But do you know how to learn as quickly and effectively as you need to in order to be successful in a world that is going much faster than it did just a few years ago?

Here's an analogy. Learning is like golf. Now, I can golf. I know this because I've done it two or three times. And every time I've golfed, I've gotten the ball into the hole. That's the idea of golf, right? But you know and I know that I don't golf well. For me to golf well, I'd need to invest some time and money into learning to be competent at the sport. I'd need to take some lessons from a competent coach, learn the principles and processes involved in a good golf swing. I'd need to acquire some good tools (clubs, shoes etc.), and then I'd need to discipline myself to practice and continuously improve. After I've done all of this, my golfing skills would inevitably improve.

So it is with learning. You can probably learn. But can you learn as well as you could? Just like you could probably dramatically improve your golf game if your livelihood depended on it, so too you can dramatically improve your learning competency – since your livelihood does depend on it. If you don't get good at learning, you won't get good at any of the other hats. Learning is the fundamental skill that enables you to acquire the competencies symbolized by the other hats.

To get better at learning, just like golf, you need to invest time and money in it, you need to have a competent

Chapter Eighteen: The Sixth Hat – Master Learner

coach work with you, you need to understand the key principles and processes, you need to acquire effective tools, and you need to discipline yourself to practice until you achieve a greater competency.

As with all the other hats, let's start with the principles. Here's the first principle: **Learning is your primary responsibility.**

One of the most common complaints I hear from salespeople goes something like this: "My company never really trained me to do this." I can understand that sentiment. From my experience, (although, as a sales trainer, I have a prejudiced perspective) very few companies do a decent job of training their salespeople. That's too bad. They would be much better off if they did spend time and money training and re-training their salespeople. But, that's not the whole story.

When I hear that complaint about training, I'll often answer, "So what?" So what that your company never trained you well? So what that they didn't spend lots of time and money on you? So what? Learning, growing, continuously improving is YOUR responsibility. If you're not performing as well as you could, it is not their fault, it's yours! Remember (chapter sixteen) my experience with the new manager in the surgical stapler company? I kept sinking deeper and deeper into financial and emotional muck – until it dawned on me that it wasn't them, it was me! It was *my responsibility* to be successful. It was my job to learn what I needed to learn to do the job well. It was totally up to me!

And when I had that great insight, it changed my attitude and my performance for the rest of my life. Once I accepted responsibility for my own actions, I realized that I could learn how to be successful. As long as I remained, in my mind, a victim of my company's omissions, I'd wallow forever in self-pity and helplessness. But when I realized it was me, not them, I was suddenly energized with the knowledge that I could change!

What a powerful truth! Learning, changing, growing, continuously improving – these are your responsibility. Becoming a Six Hat Salesperson – that's your responsibility. Yes, your company may train you, but it's still your responsibility to apply that training. When you realize the truth that it is your responsibility, it opens up an amazing future.

You can learn. And if you can learn efficiently and effectively, you can change, you can grow, you can succeed at whatever level you select. There's hope and optimism for every situation, because you can learn.

Not only is it your responsibility to learn, but it's your *primary responsibility.* As a Six Hat Salesperson, the one thing you will continue to do until you retire, is learn. That competency supports and nourishes every twig and leaf of your job. You'll need, for example, to continuously learn new products and services. Your company will develop these more rapidly than in the past. So you'll have to understand them more rapidly than in the past, and use that understanding by persuasively communicating them to your customers.

You'll need to continuously learn about the people you encounter along the way – customers, bosses, support staff, etc. They'll change in at least two ways. The individuals themselves are likely to turn over more rapidly than in the past, so you'll have to continually meet and relate to new people. But they, as individuals, will continually change and grow. Their jobs will change, their interests and needs will change. And you'll have to adjust accordingly.

Chapter Eighteen: The Sixth Hat – Master Learner

You'll need to continuously learn about the problems and opportunities your customers encounter, the applications for your products and services and the principles and processes to put all those together in a way that is effective for your customers, satisfying for you, and profitable for your company.

When you accept and internalize the truths in this principle, you're well on your way to mastering the sixth hat.

Which brings us to the next principle: **In order to get good at learning, you must invest in it.**

If you're shivering in the middle of a cold winter day, and you want to get some warmth from the fireplace, you don't expect to get the heat first, and then put in the firewood. You've got to first invest time and money in acquiring the firewood, preparing the fire, and lighting it. Then you get the result. Likewise, you don't expect learning to happen without first investing in it.

And that means making a firm commitment to invest a certain amount of time and money in your own personal growth. Too many salespeople use a happenstance approach to learning. Rather than give it quality time and devote a portion of their regular work week to it, they engage in it only in times left over from other duties. Learning becomes a hit or miss proposition.

If you were dedicated to becoming good at golf, you'd devote regular time to it, wouldn't you? And that wouldn't be ten minutes at lunch and twenty minutes at night in front of the TV. No, you'd be much more serious about it, investing a significant quantity of quality time. You may even begin every day with an hour or two on the golf course, or at the driving range.

So too, if you're going to gain mastery of this competency, you must invest a sufficient quantity of quality time.

But that's not all. You've also got to spend some money and invest in yourself. If you were going to get good at golf, you'd invest in lessons, in greens fees, in new clubs and shoes, etc. In your attempt to get good at golf you would invest thousands of dollars. But you'd be willing to pay that because you believed the payback would provide you an excellent return on that investment.

My company has a service we call The Growth Coach. It's a one-on-one or small group coaching service, designed to help executives and salespeople grow their businesses and themselves more rapidly. Early in the process we ask our participants to decide how much time and money, on a monthly basis, they are willing to invest in their own learning. Then we ask them to make a written commitment to that.

I'm often asked, "How much time and money should I be investing?" Obviously, the ultimate answer is up to you. However, we've been able to develop some basic guidelines. We generally suggest investing a minimum of five percent of the work week. If you're a typical salesperson, you work an average 49 hour week. So, you'd invest two hours a week in learning. The 5% number seems to work well for the financial side of your investment. If you take home an average of $4,000 a month, consider investing $200.00 of that in your own personal development.

Here's a simple, two-step process to help you implement these first two principles.

Chapter Eighteen: The Sixth Hat - Master Learner

 Process

 Step One. **Create a set of learning goals.**

Like so much of what we do, effective learning begins with a set of goals. Learning goals are different than performance goals. With a performance goal, you are striving to sell certain things at certain levels. The focus is on the outside world – your territory, your customers, and your sales. A learning goal, however, is something that describes an improvement you want to make in yourself. It's internal rather than external, although the evidence of it could very well be obvious to other people.

For example, you may create a sales goal of exceeding your quota by 10%. Great. Good goal. But it's a goal that describes how you perform in the outside world. You achieve this goal by influencing a sufficient quantity of other people to make decisions. You could, for example, create a learning goal that says, "I will become more adept at planning." That has nothing to do with other people, it has to do with you. The change is in you. That's a learning goal.

Here's where your new-found skill of goal-setting (see chapter fifteen) can come into place. Use that process to create a set of learning goals for yourself.

 Step Two. **Decide how much time and money you're going to invest.**

No goal is accomplished without effort. That includes learning goals. Reflect seriously, think carefully, and commit to a certain number of hours and dollars each week. Use the guidelines discussed above.

The next principle I want to address is: **To become really effective at learning, you need to acquire good tools.**

Chapter Eighteen: The Sixth Hat – Master Learner

Remember golf? If you were going to become really good at it, you'd make sure you acquired the best tools (clubs, bags, balls, etc). So it is with learning. If you're going to become really good at it, you'll need to acquire the best tools to do so.

You may be wondering what kinds of things could be learning tools. Web pages, encyclopedias, books, newsletters, etc. -- all these may come to mind. While these things could certainly be helpful, and we'll consider some of them in the next chapter, they aren't the kind of tools I have in mind.

From my perspective, ==the ultimate learning tool is *a good question!*==

That's right, a good question. Remember our discussion of questions in chapter nine? The primary function of a good question is that it directs a person's thinking. In chapter nine we made use of this aspect of questions to create sales questions in order to direct our customer's thinking, and help us understand our customers at deeper and more significant levels.

Now, we're going to use good questions to direct our own minds, to channel our own thinking, so that we can learn in a more effective manner.

The greatest teachers the world has known have used questions as one of their primary tools to help their students learn. Think of the Socratic method. Socrates facilitated learning in his students by asking them questions. A whole method of teaching developed based on that tool.

The Bible is full of examples of Jesus Christ, or God Himself, interacting with people by asking them questions. Are those questions asked in an attempt to gain information? Or, were they asked to cause the questionee to think, and thereby learn some powerful truth?

You've got the idea. A good question is like a key which unlocks the learning process. We can use good questions to unlock and open up the doors to information in three directions:
1. In the outside world,
2. In our own minds, and
3. In other people's minds.

Let's look at each.

 Questions About the Outside World.

When I use the term "outside world," I'm referring to information that exists in the external environment, outside of your mind. Here's an example of this working in a routine, daily event.

My wife and I like to spend escape weekends in Detroit. (Really, you should try it some time.) We often stay with our friends. And, like most couples, it's not unusual for Coleen and her friend to go off shopping, while Paul and I watch a sporting event on TV.

On one of these occasions, Coleen came back and reported that they had found a great muffin bakery. Truly, this place was so good that it is almost worth the three-hour drive from our home in Grand Rapids.

Let's analyze how their discovery came to happen. I'm sure that they were driving down the road, or perhaps stopping at a strip mall, and noticed the muffin bakery.

Probably, at that point, one of them said, or thought, something like this, "I wonder what that bakery is like?" To satisfy their curiosity and answer that question, they stopped in, liked what they saw, sampled the muffins, and became enthusiastic converts. Now, every time we're in the northern suburbs of Detroit, we make it a point to stop in and buy some muffins.

We changed our behavior -- we now always stop at the muffin store. We changed our behavior because of some new information we gathered – the great taste and variety of muffins. We gathered that information because someone thought and/or voiced a question. It was a question of the outside world, and it led us to new information, which led us to change our behavior. That's the definition of learning.

I recently read a story in one of the news magazines which discussed the pharmaceutical company researchers who were searching through the plants of some of the world's rainforests in order to find new compounds that would become the basis for new drugs. Perhaps a cure for the common cold will be discovered. If and when that effective new compound is discovered it will be because someone asked the right question. The compound will have been there for eons. It will have been older than mankind. But it would not have become effective unless one of those researchers asks the right question – "Is this compound effective on the common cold virus?" That question, asked of the outside world, could conceivably lead to new information, and that new information could lead to a change for all of us. It's the question that is the key that unlocks truth and power in the world around us. And once we discover that, we learn.

When Albert Einstein discovered the great law of relativity, the law itself was not new. It had been there, operating, since the creation of the universe. It took the person with the right question to discover it. Perhaps Einstein said to himself, "What is the relationship between E and MC^2?" When the right question was formulated, an incredible truth was learned. The question was the key.

When you ask questions about your accounts, your competition, the products you sell, you're asking questions of the outside world. When you ask the planning questions mentioned in chapter four regarding key account strategies, you're asking questions of the outside world.

I recently came across a great application of this principle. One of my clients, a distributor who represented dozens of manufacturers and had literally thousands of products to sell, had created a list of questions for his salespeople to ask about any new product presented to them. When they ask those questions about the product, they gained new information. And, on the basis of that new information, they made decisions about which of those products to sell and how to sell them.

Questions to Unlock Information in Our Own Minds.

The older I become, the more convinced I am that we all carry around with us far more wisdom, knowledge and insight that we ever use. Some pundits even claim that every perception we experience is stored in our minds as a memory. That would be every moment of every day, filed away in the files of our minds.

I have no way of knowing whether that is true. However, I am convinced that we are much wiser and more knowledgeable than we think we are. The missing link to unlocking the wisdom and knowledge we have is a good question. When we ask ourselves good questions, we unlock the knowledge and insights that are stored in our minds, and bring them to a level where we can implement them to make positive changes.

For example, when you ask the question I suggested in chapter fifteen "Am I doing right now the most effective thing I could be doing?" you're asking a question of yourself. You're forcing your mind to think about a certain thing.

When you take a few moments after a sales call and reflect on it, you're asking questions of yourself. Questions like "What did I do well?", "What could I have done differently?" and, "What will be the most effective next step?" cause you to think about certain things, and pull the information out of your head. You could, of course, just go on to the next sales call and never ask those questions of yourself. In that case, the information would have been stored in your mind, but never unleashed and used. It's the questions that cause that stored information to become useful to you.

Questions that Unleash Information in Other People's Minds.

If you have this vast storehouse of information in your mind, imagine how much powerful, useful information is resident in the minds of the people you encounter. Think about what you could learn if you could consistently tap into that vast treasury of powerful information. When you ask questions of your customers, your manager, and your colleagues, you are unleashing the power of the information and insights stored in their heads.

For example, when you ask your good customers the question, "What do you think we need to do in order to gain more business in this account?" you're tapping into the wisdom and insights in your customer's heads. When you ask your manager, "What can I do to improve my relationships with these two problem accounts?" you're taping into the wisdom and insights in your manager's head. When you ask one of your colleagues, "What did you do this

Chapter Eighteen: The Sixth Hat – Master Learner

week that worked very well for you?" you're learning from the experience and insights in their heads.

The world is full of powerful, useful information. You unleash that information by asking good questions. The question is the key.

But you can waste all your time by asking useless questions. For example, you could have just walked out of a miserable sales call, and thought to yourself, "Why does fate always go against me?" That question is probably not going to be worth the time it takes to think about it. A useless question.

So, let's set up some standards by which to be guided as we develop our questions.

Finally: **A good question uncovers pertinent information or useful insights, and/or moves the questioner closer to a positive future action**.

Let's look at each aspect of this principle. "Pertinent information" means information that is useful and salient to one of your learning goals. Look at the end result of the question – the information that will come in the form of an answer, and determine if that information will be useful.

For example, the question I cited above, "Why does fate always go against me" doesn't uncover any useful information. However, if you were to rephrase the question to something like this, "What am I doing that brings about a miserable sales call?" that question would bring you information that would ultimately be more usable. The fate question will not result in information that will be useful. Regardless of what answer you come up with, you won't be able to do anything about it. However, the second question may uncover information that would eventually lead you to change your behavior. You don't have the time and energy to waste on useless questions.

A new *insight* is a conclusion you draw about something you already know. For example, you may know a certain product very well. You're familiar with all its features and applications. But suppose one day your manager asks you, "What is the single most attractive aspect of that product to your larger customers?" You've never thought about that. So you think about that question for a moment, and reply, "They really like its simplicity. It's easy to use." That's an insight. You realize something that you never realized before. You always had the evidence for it, but you never realized it before. Sometimes, good questions help you discover, not new information, but new insights.

Finally, a good question moves you closer to a future, positive action. Remember, our definition of learning is dependent on behavior. ==If you don't change your behavior and act differently, you have not learned==. So, learning questions must move you to the point where you've identified a positive action you can take in the future. For example, it's one thing to ask yourself, "Why do I always make my customers irritated with me?" That would probably be good information to have. However, it wouldn't be useful unless you followed it up with another question, "What should I do differently in the future to make sure that doesn't happen again?" When you ask that question, you're moving closer to future, positive action.

As always, in order to unleash the power of this principle, you need a process. And that's what the next chapter is all about.

Chapter Nineteen:
The Menta-Morphosis™ Process

The Sixth Hat is of such importance that I've named and trademarked the primary process. Menta-Morphosis™ is my trademarked name for a specific, powerful, self-directed learning process. It's name captures the principle on which it is based: **You can change yourself and develop more rapidly by applying your mind to the task and changing your thinking.**

There is certainly nothing new about this principle. King Solomon, writing thousands of years ago in the book of Proverbs in the Bible observed, "As a man thinks, so is he." The Apostle Paul counseled the early Christians to "Be transformed by the renewing of your mind."

As always, what hinders us from applying this principle is a "how-to" process. Menta-Morphosis™ is that process. As should be no surprise to you, the process is a series of steps, each characterized by a set of questions. Illustration # 19 - 1 graphically depicts it.

The Menta-Morphosis™ Process for Continuous Self-Directed Development

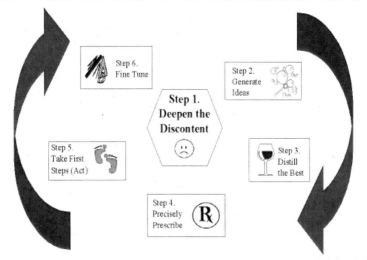

Illustration 19-1

Notice that this process is unique in that it is illustrated as a circle. It must be used over and over again. It's not a one-time task or activity, but rather a continuous way of life. Some of my clients have nicknamed this concept "Kahle's wheel."

Like all the other processes, this one also consists of a number of steps, accomplished one at a time in the sequence in which they are presented. If you follow each step precisely, and in the correct progression, you'll improve your performance -- it's guaranteed!

Let's look at each step in the process.

Step One. Deepening the Discontent.

Learning, or changing your behavior, is not easy. In fact, for adults, it is one of the most difficult challenges we have. So many things work against it. For example, we have all built habits over the years. Changing one of those

Chapter Nineteen: The Menta-Morphosis™ Process

habits is difficult. I remember the first time I drove a rental car in South Africa, where they drive on the left instead of the right side of the street. After concentrating mightily, thinking through the moves I needed to make and visualizing the car in traffic, I turned out of the parking lot directly into oncoming traffic! The habit of driving on the right side of the road was, at that point, stronger than I had anticipated it to be.

And, then of course, we all have natural inertia. It's always easier to do what we are accustomed to doing. Maintaining the status quo is always the low energy decision. It's been my observation, for example, that whenever salespeople have multiple responsibilities, and have operational tasks as well as pro-active selling to do, the operational tasks always expand to shrink the amount of time spent on pro-active selling. It's a predictable phenomenon. Why is that? Because it's easier to deal with things that come our way, to react, than it is to pro-act. Our natural inertia keeps us sitting at our desk rationalizing the things we're doing rather than out in the car creating new relationships with customers.

Understanding this, we need to do whatever we can do to improve our chances of actually making positive changes. That means that we need to load as much power into our change process as we can.

The power, energy, and motivation to change come from discontent. The people most likely to change are those who are most discontent with the status quo. And the opposite is true, also. Those least likely to change are those who are most content with their current situation. Reflect a bit on this, and you'll realize that it is true. One of the most common complaints I hear in my work as a sales consultant is the complaint from sales managers that they can't motivate some of their senior salespeople. The reason? The senior salespeople are content. They're making enough money, they've achieved many of their goals, and they see, therefore, no reason to change.

The same is true for you. If you're perfectly content, you're not going to change or grow. If you're discontent, then you'll have the power to expend the energy it takes to make changes. Therefore, if you're going to become good at the sixth hat, Master Learner, you need to ==learn how to create discontent in yourself==. And you need to make that discontent as deep and powerful as you can.

How do you create a situation of deep discontent?

★ **Start by recognizing your need to improve.**

You need to grow and improve. When you make this realization, you've entered the process. This realization can come from either of two sources – pain or gain. You either want to eliminate a situation that troubles you, (pain) or you want to gain something you don't now have. Without this internal motivation, you won't be sufficiently motivated to stretch yourself out of your comfort zones and develop new habits.

For example, you may be sick of your manager complaining about your lack of new customers. You want to do away with that pain. You are discontent with the ways things are and you want to eliminate that negative, nagging pressure.

On the other hand, you may want to add something positive to your life. You'd really like to have a new BMW. Not that your Taurus is a problem. You'd just like to have something that you don't have now. So, your discontent is channeled to a positive thing -- gaining something you don't have now.

A little thought at this point will soon make clear the significant role of goal setting in providing motivation to change and improve. When you set a goal, you create healthy discontent. In other words, you create a situation where you want something positive that you don't now have. To make this step work for you, identify some pain or gain in your life, and turn that into a goal.

It doesn't matter if its source is positive or negative. The important thing is that you have transformed it, through the goal setting process described in chapter fifteen, into a motivating goal. You've created some discontent. And this discontent is the beginning of motivation. Without it, you have no motivation. And motivation is the power that stimulates and energizes the system.

So, the beginning point in the process is your realization that you want to eliminate some pain or realize some gain in your life. I should point out that, while this system discusses sales improvement and it appears in a sales book, it can be applied to any area of your life. It doesn't matter whether you want to improve your prospecting skills or your parenting skills, your acquisition of new customers or your losing extra weight -- the system can be used for any area of personal improvement.

So, one way to attack step one is to create learning goals for yourself. But there is another, deeper way.

✦ Crystallizing your personal mission.

Here's an alternate way of creating discontent. Of the two, this is the one I prefer. There's a concept we need to discuss first, before we focus on this technique. Look at illustration #19-2. You'll recognize it from chapter fifteen. It's back to our onion analogy again. Only this time the onion is you. The layers of onion represent levels of depth in you.

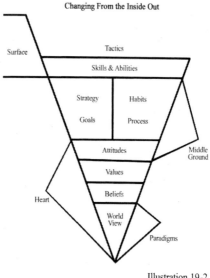

Illustration 19-2

On the very surface are your interactions with other people – your customers and prospects. These interactions are often shaped and directed by the sales tactics we've been talking about. This is the you that your customers see. For example, you may ask a customer a series of good questions, wearing the Effective Consultant hat. That series of questions is a tactic – the very surface of who you are. If you, over a period of time, develop that practice of asking questions effectively, you've created a skill. Good for you. That's important. However, in the bigger picture of everything that you are, it's the most superficial part of you.

As we peel each layer off of the onion, we go deeper into the person that you are. Just beneath the surface are the strategies you design, the goals you set, the habits you have built up over the years, and the ways you go about doing things.

Chapter Nineteen: The Menta-Morphosis™ Process

For example, let's say you ask your customer good questions. That's a tactic -- on the very surface of your being. It's where you interact with someone else.

The reason you ask questions -- the motivating force that underlies your use of that tactic -- can be one of a number of things. Perhaps it arises out of a strategic plan you created to learn more about your customer. The strategy was the deeper motivation that gave rise to the more superficial tactic.

Or, you may have developed a goal to ask four questions during the course of the day. In that case, the goal was the deeper motivation.

Or, maybe it's just your habit to always ask good questions. You're not really sure why you have that habit. In that case, the habit was the deeper issue that caused you to ask those questions.

Or, finally, the deeper issue could be a process that you've created that requires you to fill out a form with the answer to that question. Regardless, your sales behavior always arises out of one of those four motivations. You either work intentionally, with planning and forethought, as evidenced by your goals, strategies, and processes, or you work "unconsciously," through your habits and routines. These motivating forces lie just beneath the surface, but they shape your actual behavior.

Peel off that outer layer of the onion, and you'll find, at the next deepest level, your attitudes. You've heard many times about the importance of a good attitude. That's because your attitudes give rise to your habits and your goals.

When you're burdened with a depressed, pessimistic attitude, you don't set worthwhile goals or aspire to great accomplishment. The opposite is also true. When you have positive, optimistic attitudes, you naturally aspire to challenging goals, and that leads to energy and positive behavior.

If your attitude is positive, you'll feel like you can positively influence a prospect. That positive attitude can lead you to creating a goal and developing the strategy that you'll need to achieve that goal.

Back to the asking questions example. Let's say your positive attitude has led you to develop the goal of acquiring three new accounts this month. Now that you are optimistic enough to set a challenging goal, you need to create a strategy to achieve it. So, you decide on a strategy, part of which requires you to ask good questions of a certain number of prospects.

In this example, your attitude led to a goal, which led to a strategy, which led to the actions you took with your prospect. Your actions bubbled up from the inside out.

But, you're still not at the very heart of things. Underlying your attitudes are your values. Values refer to the things you hold dear and important. For example, you may value integrity, success in your job, and the well being of your spouse very highly. These values give rise to certain attitudes about those things.

Take the situation where you highly value your spouse's physical well-being. Since you value him or her so highly, you think positively about your ability to provide protection and security. Out of that attitude arises your goals and strategies.

But, you're still not finished. Underlying and supporting your values are your beliefs. For example, you may believe that it is always the husband's responsibility to support the family no matter what. This belief may be so

Chapter Nineteen: The Menta-Morphosis™ Process

deep inside you that you never really articulated it. It's just been embedded deep into your psyche.

As a result of that belief, you place a high value on the physical well-being of your spouse because, after all, it's your job to take care of that. That value leads to attitudes, which lead to goals or habits, which lead to behavior.

There is yet one layer deeper, the heart of the onion. And that is your worldview. Your worldview is comprised of your fundamental, core beliefs about the world and yourself. It's composed of the absolute deepest beliefs you hold about your purpose in life and the way in which the world functions. It differs from the beliefs above it only in degree. The worldview comprises the beginning of the spiritual part of ourselves. These beliefs shape everything above them.

For example, one person may believe that the universe is so connected that everything we do is a result of fate or destiny. Another individual may believe the opposite, that we are creatures with free will existing in a world that responds to us. A third may believe that we are the creation of a loving God -- designed for a specific purpose.

If you hold a world view that attributes everything that happens to you is controlled by fate or destiny, you'll have little interest in building positive attitudes, creating goals, developing strategies, practicing skills, and using effective tactics.

I've personally seen tribal people in developing countries who hold a world view like this. As a group, they never seem to make much progress, and many live in a life style and economic conditions that have changed little over the generations. The lack of improvement in their condition is, in my opinion, a function of their worldview. In many cases, millions of dollars of aid and years of assistance at the more superficial levels have done little. Real change won't happen until they make changes in their world-view.

This basic view of yourself and the world is usually influenced by your culture. It is often influenced by religious education, because it borders on the spiritual part of us.

Now, you're probably wondering what all this has to do with sales. Study the illustration. Notice that there is a direct relationship between the higher layers and the deeper layers. When changes are made in the deeper layers, those changes affect everything above them. Because of the nature of the onion, a small change made deep down in a person will affect almost everything above it.

If you change your attitudes, you'll change your strategy, habits and actions. Change your values and your beliefs, and you can't help but change your attitudes. Modify your worldview, and everything above it will change.

Now, suppose you were to crystallize one part of your worldview – the image you have of yourself. Suppose you were to see yourself as a unique entity with a unique place and purpose. And suppose you were to think about this unique purpose and project forward to the point that you had become almost everything you were capable of becoming, doing exactly the work you were meant to do, using the unique combination of competencies and life experiences you have accumulated along the way. And finally, suppose you were able to crystallize and articulate that vision of yourself. Would that vision of who you could become provide sufficient discontent to power your self-directed development?

Chapter Nineteen: The Menta-Morphosis™ Process

Of course it would. And that brings us to the second way to deepen the discontent. Uncover and articulate your vision of who you are meant to become, resolve the question of your purpose in life. Keeping that vision in front of you provides the power of discontent simply because you are not now who or what you want to be. And that gap between who you were meant to become and who you are now is the discontent that powers your efforts.

I once taught an intense 10-week sales training program in which the first week was given to a discussion of world-views, and the first assignment was to write a statement of your purpose in life.

Why bother? Because the more completely you resolve the deeper issues, the more likely it will be that you will have congruence, not conflict, in all the layers above. I have never met a consistently successful professional salesperson who hadn't calmly and confidently resolved the deeper issues. I have met hundreds of salespeople who have had short-term success, sometimes spectacularly so, but whose lack of deeper grounding spun them out of control, crashing and burning in some self-defeating behavior.

A couple years ago, a friend of mine developed a seminar that was so well received it was growing into a movement. The seminar had to do with how to develop a personal mission statement – a clear, articulate description of your unique place and purpose.

To add power to the process of making significant, long-lasting, permanent changes in your results, resolve the deeper issues in your life.

When you're finished with this step, you've answered the question, "Why should I learn?" You've loaded some power into the learning process.

Step Two. Generate Good Ideas.

Now it's time to generate some ideas. You have your goals, but you haven't developed ways to reach them. That's where "good ideas" come in. A good idea is a possibility, some way you can achieve all or part of your goals.

The next step in the Menta-Morphosis ™ process is generating, and collecting multitudes of good ideas. Good ideas are all around you. You only need to learn how to recognize and capture them.

Generating these ideas is an essential step. Think about it. If your goal is to change yourself in some way, you must act differently. Before you can act differently, you must decide how to act. Before you can decide how to act, you must have some ideas of actions you can take that will bring you positive results. So, you must develop some ideas before you can act differently. Here's an illustration of how this works:

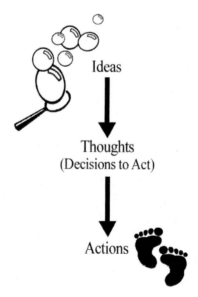

Illustration 19-3

Chapter Nineteen: The Menta-Morphosis™ Process

The process starts with good ideas. So, generating good ideas -- ideas about how you can make changes and act differently in order to reach your goals -- is a necessary step.

You can generate good ideas in two basic ways:
1. Injecting yourself into learning opportunities.
2. Reflecting on past experiences.

Let's explore each way.

Injecting yourself into learning opportunities.

A learning opportunity is an experience whereby you come into contact with new information or you develop new insights. Learning opportunities can take many forms. Here's a list of some of the most common:

* Seminars and workshops
* Classes sponsored by educational institutions
* Small-group discussions with your peers
* Company meetings
* Coaching sessions
* Conversations with your bosses or managers
* Books
* Audio and video tapes
* Articles in periodicals
* Articles and web pages on the Internet
* Educational television programs
* Conversations with friends and associates
* Telephone conferences
* Video conferences
* Watching a role model
* Talking with a mentor

For the rest of your working life, you'll need to regularly inject yourself into some of these learning opportunities. Your company may provide you with some opportunities. But you shouldn't rely solely on the company to provide learning opportunities for you. If you're going to be in charge of your own learning, you must take the initiative yourself. Remember the earlier principle: **Learning is your primary responsibility.**

⭐ **Turning goals into questions.**

One of the best ways to begin is to turn your learning goals into questions. For example, one of your learning goals may be, "To get along better with my branch manager." If you started to work at that goal, you'd naturally develop some questions. You may think:

* What can I do differently to get along with my branch manager?
* What is the best way for me to get along with my branch manager?

Each of these questions:
1) focus on things you control.
2) are pointed toward the future.
3) directly relate to the goal.

This process of turning a goal into a major question or two will help you to select appropriate learning opportunities. For example, if you decide that you want to improve your relationship with your branch manager, you may begin to look for a seminar on "interpersonal skills." Or you may look for an opportunity to talk with your peers on how they do it, or maybe even a conversation with a mentor about it.

When you've identified and entered into a learning opportunity, it's time to use that opportunity to generate ideas.

Chapter Nineteen: The Menta-Morphosis™ Process

 Generating good ideas from learning opportunities.

Let's assume that you're reading a book as one of your learning opportunities. Remember, the purpose of reading the book is simple: to generate good ideas and/or to stimulate new insights. It's nice that the book looks good on your bookshelf, impresses your friends, and gives you something to talk about in social conversations. All of that is extraneous. Nice -- but not important.

If you chose the book well, it should provide you some information or insights that you didn't have before. That's good, but only a means to an end. New information is helpful, as long as it leads to good ideas. Remember the definition of a "good idea." It's an idea that focuses on the future and describes potential behavior--things you can <u>do</u> differently. If the information you've acquired doesn't lead to good ideas, it's not worth the time it takes to ingest that information. Information or insights that don't lead to good ideas are impotent. The only useful purpose for the time you spend reading that book, or involved in any learning opportunity, is the generation of good ideas.

So, the question is, "How do you generate good ideas?"

The answer is to ask yourself questions. As you ask yourself questions, you prompt your mind to reflect on the ideas and content in the book. That thought process leads to good ideas. It really is that simple.

Here are two sets of questions to ask. Create a discipline of asking yourself these questions after you read any section of the book, attend a seminar, listen to a tape, or engage in any learning opportunity.

1. *In this section, were there any insights to be gained?* (Remember the definition of an insight, from the previous chapter.)

2. *How does that insight apply to my situation?*
3. *What could I do differently?*

This series of questions asks you to first identify insights, and then generate ideas from those insights. The diagram of the process looks like this:

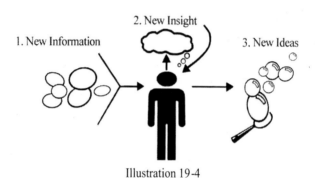

Illustration 19-4

As an alternative, try skipping the first two questions, and leaping right to the heart of the matter with this question:

* *Did this section give me any ideas about ways in which I can do things differently?*

This is a simpler approach and works for some people, some of the time.

Here's one more variation on the technique. Ask yourself the questions *before* you read the section. This technique programs your subconscious mind and directs it to look for the answers to the questions. When you ask yourself the questions above, you will find yourself coming up with answers as you read. Just make sure that you allow yourself time at the end of each section to reflect on that section a bit, and wait for the answers to appear.

This process of asking yourself questions is the basic technology for generating ideas regardless of the type of

Chapter Nineteen: The Menta-Morphosis™ Process

learning opportunity. You ask the same questions whether you are reading a book, attending a seminar, in a discussion group, or taking part in a teleconference.

Let's go back to our example of reading a book. As you read, you stop momentarily after each section, and ask yourself the questions listed above. For example, you may be reading a book on "interpersonal skills," and the book talks about adjusting to different personality styles. You realize that your branch manager is one kind of personality style, and you're another. Good! You've acquired an *insight*. Now, you think some more about it, asking yourself the question, "How does that insight apply to my situation?" You think, "That might be part of the problem, I want him to be like me, and it irritates me that he doesn't act or think the way I do."

Now ask yourself the last question, "What could I do differently?" You answer yourself, "I should try to appreciate his style as a complement to mine." Good! That's a good idea.

Now, before you go any further, capture that good idea. Write it down. Remember the image of the bubble wand? Wave it through the air and layers of bubbles appear. With the right combination of materials and motion, you can use the bubble wand to fill the air with bubbles. Good ideas are like these bubbles. The right combination of materials (your experiences) and motions (your thought processes) will result in dozens of good ideas.

After you've captured the good idea, continue on with the book or the learning experience in which you're involved.

As you do that, you'll develop a whole file of good ideas. You'll work with them later. Right now, the important thing is that you use your learning opportunities to generate good ideas. Whenever you generate one, stop and write it down.

❊ The serendipity approach to generating good ideas.

So far, we've been discussing a *targeted approach* to generating good ideas. In other words, you've decided beforehand what you wanted to learn, planned for appropriate learning opportunities, and created ideas from those experiences. That proactive approach is necessary.

But not all learning takes place in that way. Sometimes we learn in less targeted ways, in ways I call "serendipity." The dictionary defines *serendipity* as the "process of making happy chance discoveries." We can make happy, chance learning discoveries.

Here's how it works. Let's say you just had a very good conversation with your branch manager. You enjoyed it and felt good about it. You and he finally seemed to communicate. After the experience, as you're driving home, you mentally review the conversation. Often, that's as far as we normally take it. But suppose you were to reflect on the experience you just had, and asked yourself the question, "What was it that made this such a good experience?" As you think through the answer to that question, you come up with these things:

* We both found something we thought was funny, and laughed about it together.
* I didn't feel the usual tension I feel with him.
* I wasn't looking for something to find fault with.

One more question for you to reflect on. "Does that experience prompt any ideas about how you should act in the future?"

As you think about that question, you come up with these ideas:

* I should find something we can laugh about together.
* I should not look for things to find fault with, or object to.

Do you know what you just did? You generated some good ideas. Only this time, the good ideas came from an experience that you had, one from which you didn't necessarily intend to learn. It was a "happy, chance discovery."

The primary thinking technology used in serendipity learning is the process of "reflecting." Reflecting is simply the process of thinking about your experiences, and generating ideas from those experiences. You engage in the process of reflection by simply asking yourself questions, and developing the answers. You can use this simple process whenever you have an experience that seems particularly successful or unsuccessful.

Reflect on it by asking yourself those questions:
* What was it that made this so (successful, unsuccessful)?
* What can I learn from that?
* What ideas does this give me for the future?
* What could I do differently in the future?

Not only can you reflect on a specific incident or experience, you can also reflect on a much wider set of experiences. Let's go back to the same goal, "To achieve a great relationship with my branch manager." You can choose to reflect on your life! Set aside some time, and focus your thinking. Here are some questions you could ask yourself in order to help generate some good ideas.

"Have I ever been in a similar situation-- where I didn't get along with someone in authority?"

> "Have I ever been in a situation where I was the manager or person in authority, and didn't get along with someone?"
>
> "What happened in each of those situations? Did the relationship get better, or worse? What did the person being managed do to improve or detract from the relationship?"
>
> "If that were true of that situation, would it be true of this situation?"
>
> "What can I do, based on what I've already experienced, that might work in this current situation?"

When you ask yourself that last question, you may well generate some ideas that you can use to achieve your goal. Got the idea? That's how reflection works. You may want to schedule some time for reflection on each of your goals.

Now, you have two means of generating good ideas: 1) injecting yourself into learning opportunities and 2) serendipity. The end result of all of these is a list of good ideas.

Once you're comfortable generating good ideas, it's time to move to the next step - using these techniques to help you reach your goals.

One last thought. It's amazing how our minds work. Once you give it the job of creating good ideas, your subconscious mind will accept that task and begin to work on it. When it has done some subconscious reflection, it may well spit out the good ideas it created. You may, therefore, be driving in your car, watching TV, reading a good book, or barbecuing for the family when a good idea will strike you. Don't let it go. Immediately write it down. If you don't write it down immediately, you will probably lose it and never capture it again.

Your job now is to distill several good ideas out of that information. Which brings us to the next step in the process.

Step Three. Distill the Best.

The easy part is over. If you go no further than this point, and that's what most people do, you've just wasted your time. You're like the person who makes New Year's resolutions but never follows through on them. You're satisfied with good ideas and vague intentions. If you want to get serious, you must progress through the rest of the process.

This step requires you to select some of the good ideas that you wish to implement. Sort through the ideas and identify the best of those. I call this "distilling the best." This process of *distilling the best*, like all the other thinking/learning processes, is a matter of asking yourself questions, and developing the answers. Sift through your ideas by asking yourself these questions:

1. Which one or two of these ideas could make the *fastest* impact on achieving your goals?
2. Which one or two of these ideas could make the *biggest* impact on achieving your goals?
3. Which one or two of these ideas would be the *easiest* for you to implement?
4. Which one or two ideas are you *most passionate* about?

I suggest that you look over the list and pick no more than three. For example, let's say you read a book on sales -- this one! As a result, you created a list of good ideas.

Your list looks like this:
* Get better organized.
* Create account and personal profiles.
* Ask better questions.
* Focus on knowing my customers deeper and broader.
* Develop creative proposals.
* Implement "learned optimism."
* Create annual and quarterly personal goals.
* Create monthly strategic plans for my "A" accounts.
* Work at continuous improvement.

Now, even I'll admit that this is an ambitious agenda. Realistically, you're not going to be able to implement all of these ideas right away. So, you prioritize by selecting the three good ideas that you think will have the greatest potential effect on your performance. Let's consider the following examples:
* Get better organized.
* Ask better questions.
* Create monthly strategic plans for my "A" accounts.

What about the rest of the ideas you generated? Are they worthless? Not at all -- they're just not the highest priority at this moment. Create another file for yourself. Label this one, "Good ideas." Then put your list and all the supporting notes for those ideas into that file. When you've completed "Kahle's wheel," and you have successfully implemented your current high priority list, they'll still be there for you to consider again.

When you have arrived at this point, you've successfully completed step three.

As you may have surmised, this step of distilling the best is a process that needs to be repeated on a regular basis. You can do it after every major learning experience on a regular basis. Try to set aside some time at least once a month to devote to this process, you've completed the next step. You've *distilled the best* of your ideas.

Step Four. Precisely Prescribe.

Here's the step that separates the serious learners from those who just toy with the process. This is hard work. This step requires you to move from good ideas and vague intentions to specific commitments to change your behavior in precise ways.

To bridge that gap, you must translate each of your good ideas into precise prescriptions by rewriting each idea, beginning with the words, 'I will...".

In the example, let's work on the good idea, "avoiding finding fault with my branch manager." Rewrite it to read, " I will avoid finding fault with my branch manager." Sounds good, but it's a little too vague to really help you change. You need to rewrite it to make it more specific. "I will avoid finding fault with my branch manager every day. I will dismiss negative thoughts as soon as they come into my head, and I will never voice them to anyone."

That's much better because it's more specific. It's achievable and realistic. But you're not home yet. Make sure that your statement meets two criteria:
1. It expresses behavior that someone else can witness.
2. At the end of the day, you can ask yourself whether or not you did what you said you were going to do, and you can answer that question with a simple "yes" or "no."

Let's go back to the example. You have written the statement, "I will...." Does that express behavior that someone else can witness? Can a tiny, invisible manager who rides around on your shoulder all day witness you do that? He couldn't see your thoughts, but he could observe your words so, this statement counts.

So, your statement now meets the first criterion.

Now, consider your statement in light of the second criterion. Is it something that, at the end of the day, you can ask yourself, "Did I do this," and answer yes or no?

At the end of the day, can you say "Yes, I did it, or "No, I didn't?" Yes, you can. So, now your statement meets the second criterion.

Now, you're ready for the next step.

Like the previous process, this step of *"precisely prescribing"* should be repeated regularly. Try to do so at least once a month as well as after a particularly affective learning experience.

When you have completed this step, you will have succeeded at the crucial step of translating your good ideas and vague intentions into precise prescriptions for your future behavior. You've completed one of the most difficult tasks in my system. You're now ready for the next step.

Step Five. Act.

This is the hardest part of the whole system. It's just so easy to keep on doing the things that we've always done. We're comfortable with it. But, if you're going to make any progress, if you're serious about learning and growing, then you must act. You must stretch yourself and do something that you may never have done before. You'll push yourself outside of your comfort zone to the risky area of behaving in some new way.

This is almost always difficult and laden with fear and anxiety. You'll make the task easier by following the Menta-Morphosis ™ process to this point. Doing so will establish the logical reasons to change and try something new. It will also define your new behavior very precisely and thus make it easier to do. You've stacked the deck on your side to make it easier for you to improve.

All you have to do now is do it. Easier said than done. Here's some helpful techniques that will help you translate your ideas into action. First publish your prescriptions. That means that you share your intentions with someone else. The fact that you've made your prescriptions public, that other people know, adds pressure on you to actually do what you say you're going to do. It helps, however, if you also have others who are aware of what you're intending to do. It makes it easier to act.

Then just do it. The first time is the most difficult. Once you've done the thing once, you'll find it much easier to do it again. And then again, and so on until you've repeated this new behavior enough to make it a habit.

Here's a technique that will help you focus on turning your new behaviors into actions. Look at illustration #19-6. It is a form on which to keep track of your progress. Use it like this.

SALES HABIT BUILDER

Month:_____

Activity	1	2	3	4	5	6	7	8	9	10	11	12	13	14	15	16	17	18	19	20	21	22	23	24	25	26	27	28	29	30	31

Illustration 19-6

Turn each of your precise prescriptions into one or two word descriptions. For example, your prescription about getting along with your branch manager reads, "*I will avoid finding fault with my branch manager every day. I will dismiss negative thoughts as soon as they come into my head, and I will never voice them to anyone.*" Turn it into a one or two word description, *"No Negatives."* Write that description in the wide column on the left.

Now, at the end of each day, ask yourself this question. "Did I do today, what I said I was going to do?" In other words, did you eliminate all negative thoughts about your branch manager today? If you can honestly answer "Yes," then mark an X in the space for today's date. If the answer is "no," then put a zero in the space.

Some behaviors are things that you can work on daily. That's what the 1-31 blocks are for. Others are things that you repeat weekly. Use the wider (5 spaces per month) to record your progress on those.

Repeat this short step every day. The thirty seconds or so that it takes each day to do this will keep your prescriptions firmly planted in your mind, and keep you focused on making the changes you said you were going to make.

When you have acted by doing, a number of times, the things that you said you were going to do, then it's time to move on to the next step.

Step Six: Fine-Tune.

Generally, you don't get it right the first few times you try something new. That means that you must refine what you're doing, making fine-tuning changes in your actions in order to bring about the results you want. In fact, you may have to repeat this process several times,

Chapter Nineteen: The Menta-Morphosis™ Process

continually trying, then making small revisions and trying again, until you finally achieve that kind of behavior for which you're looking. Think of golf, as an example. How many fine-tuning adjustments does it take to come up with the perfect swing?

The process for doing so is similar to the reflection process for generating ideas. After you've had the experience of trying some new behavior, you reflect on your experience by asking yourself questions. Use these questions:
* Did I do what I said I was going to do?
* Why or why not?
* What happened as a result of my actions?
* What can I learn from this?
* What should I do differently the next time?

As you ask yourself these questions, you focus your mind on your behavior and the results of your actions. You develop answers, and those answers can serve as ideas and insights. As you review the answers to your questions, decide what you're going to do differently the next time by distilling the best of the ideas you come up with, and then precisely prescribing your action.

You're making fine tuning changes, small adjustments that move you closer to the competency for which you're striving. Continue this process of acting and refining until you feel that you've arrived at a degree of competency with which you're happy.

At that point, you can honestly say that you've learned. You've changed your behavior in a positive way. You're a different, more capable, more competent person.

And, perhaps more importantly, you've learned a process you can use to accelerate your learning for the rest of your life. You can now use this process and principles, the sixth hat, to implement all of the other hats. But that's only one of dozens of applications. You can use this same process to grow and develop in every area of your life. Whether you want to be a better manager, salesperson, or spouse, a more effective parent, a better friend, or a more sensitive spirit, you can use Menta-Morphosis™ to fuel your growth. That's the power of the Menta-Morphosis ™ process. Once you learn the system, you can use it over and over again, forever. The Menta-Morphosis ™ process should serve you well forever.

Now, it's up to you to continue.

❋ Trying on the Hat

The amount of material contained in this hat isn't as great is that in some of the other hats. However, the impact this set of competencies can have on your career and your sales performance is immeasurable. Let's review...

We discussed these principles:
1. **Learning is the process of taking in new information, or developing new insights, and then changing your behavior in positive ways as a result.**
2. **Learning is your primary responsibility.**
3. **In order to get good at learning, you must invest in it.**
4. **To become really effective at learning, you need to acquire good tools.**
5. **A good question uncovers pertinent information or useful insights, and/or moves the questioner closer to a positive future action.**
6. **You can change yourself and develop more rapidly by applying your mind to the task and changing your thinking.**

Chapter Nineteen: The Menta-Morphosis™ Process

There was one master process that incorporates all of these principles: The Menta-Morphosis ™ process. Becoming a master of continuous, systematic, self-directed learning requires you to learn and use that process. It will enable you to change effectively and efficiently. Master it, and you'll be able to use it, over and over for the rest of your life. It will help accelerate your career growth as it helps you grow and add new competencies.

Unfortunately, there is no shortcut. The way to begin trying on this hat is to dig in at step one -- *Deepening the Discontent*. Set aside some time in the next week or so to develop your career and learning goals, to commit some resources to them, and to think deeply about the rewards and consequences of achieving them. You should repeat this step at least once a year.

When you've created those goals and made some commitments for resources, move on to the next step, *Generating Ideas*.

As soon as you can, make a commitment for some learning opportunity. It may be a seminar or a tape or another book. Review the list of typical learning opportunities, and get involved in *something*.

Then, as you experience the learning opportunity, focus on collecting usable ideas. Create a big list. You may even want to categorize them, and file them away in an electronic or manila folder. I use a special post-it to write down my good ideas, and then file them in one of about eight different categories.

The third step is to *Distill the Best* of those ideas, a process of categorizing, editing and prioritizing. So, after you have some ideas in your list, review them and select those two or three that you want to focus on initially.

Step four requires you to translate those selected ideas into *Precise Prescriptions* for your behavior. Review this chapter to show you how to do that.

Step five requires you to *Act* in those new and positive ways--a never-ending daily challenge.

Step six involves *Fine-Tuning* and repeating its new behaviors until you reach a level of competency. This process of reviewing your actions and their consequences is really a repetition of steps 2, 3, 4 and 5. It should be a formal, monthly discipline, but you can engage in it more frequently.

That brings you back where you started. Start the whole process over again.

✦ Wearing the Hat

If anything characterizes masters of the sixth hat, it is rapid, continuous personal development. When you've continually implementing this hat, you'll be moving forward in your career more rapidly, seeing more success in your sales performance, and even living a more fulfilling life. Remember, the Menta-Morphosis ™ process is not just for sales. Use it to grow in every area of your life.

When you're fully implementing the competencies of this hat, you'll be devoting a generous amount of time and resources to your own personal development. The Menta-Morphosis™ process will become a regular part of your routine.

Here's a list of the steps and their recommended frequency:

    1. Deepening the Discontent - Annually
    2. Generating Ideas - Daily
    3. Distilling the Best - Monthly
    4. Precisely Prescribing - Monthly

5. Acting - Daily
6. Refining - Monthly

As you repeat the process, you will find yourself becoming a master of systematic, self-directed learning, the Sixth Hat. And that is the ultimate success skill for the Information Age and the ultimate path to continuously taking your performance up-a-notch!

Chapter Twenty:
Using the Six•Hats to Take Your Performance Up-A-Notch

Challenge: Just when I get comfortable with some method or product, my company changes it. It seems like I'm in a constant state of confusion. I could do a lot better job of selling if I had some stability from my company.

I can empathize. Countless numbers of salespeople have confided very similar thoughts to me at seminars and training programs. Compensation plans change, territories evolve, inside staff turn over, new programs and products come and go – it's hard to keep focused when the internal support you count on seems as sure and solid as a bowl of Jell-O.

Unfortunately, this is probably not a temporary phenomenon. Let's go all the way to where we began, with an understanding that the world around us is changing at an ever increasing rate. In all likelihood, your company is doing so, also. Even if they aren't today, they will probably be doing so tomorrow.

It's not going to go away. This constant change, both inside your organization as well outside, is the hallmark of the Information Age. You don't have many options in dealing with this change.

You can drop out. Refuse to change, refuse to adjust, and give up. Maybe you would be happier living on welfare.

"OK," you're thinking, "that's really drastic. Certainly there are other options."

Sure, you can find employment that isn't so demanding. But the issue of rapid change won't go away. You can't escape it. Ask anyone in the jobs you might consider if things are changing rapidly for them. Listen to them say the same things you are thinking. In any job you get, you're going to need to deal with rapid change. So, if you want to not deal with rapid change, you've got to drop out of the economic system.

But, you might not want to do that. What other options do you have?

You could live, for awhile, in denial. Nod your head at sales meetings, offer lip service to your manager, and go about doing your job the way that you've always done it, pretending that you can get by without changing. But, how long will you last? In most organizations, that approach will catch up with you in a few months. So, unless you've got alternate employment arranged within that period of time, denial isn't a viable long-term strategy.

Your last option is really your best option. It comes down to this – you've got to change. You've got to be able to be flexible, to adjust, to change the way you do your job, to change the tools you use, to change your approaches and your methods. If you're going to survive and prosper, you must become a master of personal change.

At my presentations and sales seminars, I am almost always asked a version of this question by a manager or business owner: "How do I get my salespeople to change." Or, there will be a variation of that, "How tough should I be in insisting my salespeople change?"

Chapter Twenty: Using the Six Hats to Take Your Performance Up-A-Notch

I often respond with this real life experience of one of my clients. After studying the issue of sales force automation thoroughly, my client decided to automate his sales force of six outside salespeople. He developed his own contact management, sales forecasting software, and invested in lap top computers for each salesperson. His requirement of them was that they type in a two-minute sales call report after each sales call, answering several specific questions.

Recognizing that some of them didn't know how to type, he offered to pay for typing classes for them, and required that they complete those classes in the next eight months.

Four of the salespeople quietly -- not arrogantly, not boisterously, not confrontationally -- just quietly decided not to do so. Their position was this; "We're professional salespeople. We make our living selling. We're not clerks. We don't need to type. Since when do salespeople need to know how to type?"

My client's position was this: "Since when do salespeople need to know how to type? Since now. This is how we're going to go to market. This is how we're going to do sales in this company. If you don't learn to type, you can't do sales the way we do it."

The net result was the four salespeople were replaced. And I wholeheartedly supported him in that decision.

Here's why. The need to change and grow and develop is the fundamental success skill in the Information Age. If someone or ones fight you on this issue, they will continue to defy you on others. Today it's the computer, tomorrow it's a new compensation plan, then it's a new product line, program or approach to the market, a new territory or a new presentation. It doesn't matter what it is.

The underlying skill, the operational attitude is the "ability and propensity to change." So, in dealing with this issue of rapid internal change, or for that matter rapid external change, your only really effective option is to learn to change also.

The Six Hats are your keys to continuous success in a rapidly changing world. The principles are the anchors you can count on to stabilize and support your sales efforts for the rest of your career. The processes provide the bridges from your understanding of the principle to effectively implementing them in your life. The combination of the two will empower you to successfully adjust to changing circumstances, no matter what they are.

Use the Six Hats wisely. Stay the path to continuous improvement, daily taking your performance up a notch!

About the Author . . .

Dave is a consultant and speaker who helps his clients grow their sales and develop their people. Specializing in business-to-business selling situations, Dave creates effective sales systems and helps salespeople take their performance up a level.

He's acquired his message through real-life experience. Dave has been the number one salesperson in the country for two different companies in two distinct industries.

As the general manager of a start-up company, Dave directed that company's growth from $10,000 in monthly sales to over $200,000 in just 38 months.

Dave annually presents over 75 seminars and training programs. He has spoken in 46 states and 7 countries, published over 600 articles, writes a weekly sales Ezine, and has authored 7 books and 32 multi-media training programs.

He holds a B.A. degree from the University of Toledo, and a Master's from Bowling Green State University.

He and his wife live in Grand Rapids, MI, where he is a father, a stepfather, an adoptive father, a foster father, and a grandfather.

Dave is a member of the Author's guild, the Christian Businessman's Committee, and the American Society for Training and Development.

He can be reached at:
The DaCo Corporation
P.O. Box 230017
Grand Rapids, MI 49503
(800) 331-1287
(616) 451-9377
(616) 451-9412 facsimile
info@davekahle.com
www.DaveKahle.com

Dave Kahle is available to:

- Speak at your conference or convention.

- Create customized sales training programs for your outside sales force, inside sales force, or sales managers.

- Provide "Up-A-Notch" seminars.

- Consult with you on issues relating to sales productivity.

For more information:

    Call: 1-800-331-1287

    Write: The DaCo Corporation
                  P.O. Box 230017
                  Grand Rapids, MI 49523

    Fax: 616-451-9412

    E-Mail: *Dave@davekahle.com*

    Website: *www.davekahle.com*

Join Dave's Thinking About Sales newsletter, a monthly e-mailed source for education, motivation and inspiration from Dave Kahle. Visit us at *www.davekahle.com*.